THE ROLE OF A GREAT GAME DESIGNER

THE ROLE OF A GREAT GAME DESIGNER

RICHARD CARRILLO

Copyright © 2021 by Richard Carrillo

All rights reserved. No part of this publication may be reproduced, stored or transmitted in any form or by any means, electronic, mechanical, photocopying, recording, scanning, or otherwise without written permission from the publisher. It is illegal to copy this book, post it to a website, or distribute it by any other means without permission.

Richard Carrillo asserts the moral right to be identified as the author of this work.

First edition
ISBN: 9798542127699

Front cover design by Katya Garipova

Full cover, illustrations, and interior design by Mahadev Rojas Torres

Edited by Sarah Lane (pickletack.com)

For my father, who put everything aside to raise two sons who will always be grateful.

Contents

PREFACE 9

PART ONE: Definitions
Chapter 1: DEFINING *GAME* 23

Chapter 2: DEFINING *GAME DESIGN* 39

Chapter 3: ENTER THE GAME DESIGNER 57

PART TWO: Process
Chapter 4: THE GAME DESIGN PROCESS 79

Chapter 5: IDENTIFY THE PROBLEM 85

Chapter 6: BUILD GOALS 93

Chapter 7: MAXIMIZE IDEAS 99

Chapter 8: DESIGN THE SOLUTION 111

Chapter 9: PROTOTYPE THE SOLUTION 119

Chapter 10: PLAYTEST THE SOLUTION 125

Chapter 11: ANALYZE PLAYTEST RESULTS 133

Chapter 12: FINALIZE OR ITERATE 143

PART THREE: Skills
Chapter 13: CORE SKILLS 151

Chapter 14: CORE HARD SKILLS 155

Chapter 15: CORE SOFT SKILLS 189

Chapter 16: THE ROLE OF A GREAT GAME DESIGNER 209

AFTERWORD	221
ACKNOWLEDGMENTS	223
SNEAK PEAK OF *BOOK 2: DESIGN PERSPECTIVES*	225
About the Author	235

PREFACE

This book is for game designers of all experience levels and for the teams, developers, and support staff they work with. It's meant to showcase the reality of what game designers really do (or should be doing) and sheds light on some widespread misconceptions of the job, misconceptions like "Game designers control the game," "Game designers know best," and the dreaded "Coolest idea wins." These misconceptions can cause designers to focus on the wrong values, be difficult to work with, or create production teams that don't know how to utilize their design teams effectively.

I wrote this book to be an easy-to-read, practical guide for the following people:

Game Designers. This book will discuss what game designers really own and the skills they need to be successful. Although anyone can design games, not everyone is a game designer. What distinguishes those two is the team. Game designers, unlike people who happen to design games, are a part of passionate development teams. Working successfully alongside such a team is as important as the game design itself. In this book as we discuss how to successfully drive the gameplay experience from vision to final product, we'll also dive deeper into the skills required to inspire the team and build belief in the design among teammates.

Future Game Designers. For those passionate about becoming game designers, I have a few words of wisdom: *Game design isn't about your game ideas*. If you want to become a game designer because you believe you have great game ideas, then you'll be truly disappointed with the actual job. Instead you'll find the job is about your critical thinking and ability to design. In short, it has to do with how you turn the millions of ideas already out in the world and the thousands of ideas the dev team already has into solid designs that solve the current problem, fit the vision's goals, and enhance the gameplay experience. In this book we'll further discuss the difference between ideas and designs as well as dive deeper into the true day-to-day job of a game designer.

Teams/Support. For everyone else already in game development but not on the design team, this book can help you better understand how games are structured and how to ensure your craft enhances the game's vision and the gameplay experience. I also give you the task of sharing the knowledge in this book with the game designers on your teams. Why? Because it's the game designer's job to inspire you. Great design means nothing without a team driving their passion into the product. The team is the designer's first customer. The moment they forget that, morale starts to fall and the game starts to suffer. But that doesn't mean the customer is always right. In this book I'll showcase what designers are expected to own and how they should always turn to the team for ideas and feedback.

Whether you're new to game design, looking to hone your skills, or dreaming to completely restructure your design team's philosophy, there's something here for you. My goal with this book is to raise the role of game designer to a higher standard across the video game industry.

✹ ✹ ✹ ✹

My Background

I started my career in May of 2005 as a Production Intern at EA Tiburon in Orlando, Florida. Fifteen years later I still wonder how it all happened. But more importantly I look back trying to determine what knowledge and skills led me to become the AAA Creative Director I am today. Each step along the way I learned something different, something powerful.

EA Tiburon

Tiburon is the powerhouse studio that ships the Madden franchise. But that May I was joining the NCAA Football '07 team, which was in pre-production.

I got the internship thanks to a job fair at the University of Illinois at Urbana-Champaign where I was getting a degree in Computer Science. My whole goal was to enter the video game industry, but if I couldn't then at least I wouldn't starve with a CS degree. I walked up to the Electronic Arts booth wearing my best suit (my only suit) and my cherished *Spy vs. Spy* tie. The casually dressed reps at the booth made fun of the suit but loved the tie. I got the interview.

What I hadn't revealed yet is that I didn't want to be a programmer. I wanted to design. Before the interview I researched Electronic Arts and the industry as much as I could. I didn't really know the job titles so I wanted to make sure I understood what I was looking for and could ask the right questions. When the interview came, they opened with the standard "Tell me about yourself" inquiry, and I explained that I didn't want to be a programmer. My goal was to design, but more importantly I wanted a producer role at EA where I could use my skills in design, programming, and art to bring everyone together and ship a great product. *Industry Lesson 1: Always focus on what you can offer them during interviews.*

Most EA studios at the time didn't have the game designer role since a lot of studios were working on sports titles. Instead, producers filled in where needed to oversee production and quality. *Lesson 2: Know the company you're interviewing for and showcase your research during the interview.* It shows you're passionate and interested in them. The interviewer quickly switched up the questions and we had a fun conversation. I was in!

What I witnessed that summer at EA Tiburon was a fine-tuned machine. The football games they developed were annual releases. They knew their product better than any studio I've ever come across. And they loved it. During my internship I was part of brainstorms, feature design, and capturing mood video footage, and I made a lot of friends along the way (especially with the HR staff that ran the internship program). *Lesson 3: It's not what you know. It's not who you know. It's who knows you.*

I soaked up as much knowledge as I could in the three months I was there and was sad for it to end.

EA Chicago

During my final semester at college I used the contacts I made at EA Tiburon to interview for a full-time position with Electronic Arts Chicago. I received an offer to be a dev tester at the studio. It seemed like a step backward, but the General Manager had also started his career as a tester. He felt that every producer needed to start at this role to get a deeper understanding of game development. I was bummed, but I accepted. It was a foot in the door and a full-time job. In May of 2006, I officially started my career in the gaming industry. *Lesson 4: Get in and work hard!*

EA Chicago was run on raw passion. They had just shipped *Fight Night Round 3* and were now developing *Def Jam: ICON*.

The studio had around 150 employees, and for a while I was the only dev tester. The GM was right. After a year of build management, testing, IT support, and any other odd job they needed, I understood every person's role in that building. Soon after shipping *Def Jam: ICON,* I moved up to Assistant Producer on a new unannounced project at the studio. Sadly, like most game projects, it never shipped.

While at EA Chicago I learned two other big lessons. One was from the Chief Technical Officer who told me that ideas were worthless (or maybe he said they were worth pennies). At the time, I felt he couldn't be more wrong. Ideas drove everything, right? It took me many years to finally understand what he was saying and how right he was. I discuss this later on in this book.

The other lesson was from GM. He offered many lessons but the biggest one I learned just by watching him lead. For a while I called it Salesmanship, his ability to get anyone excited about anything. He got the team pumped about features and the press pumped about games. I would later call this The Ability to Inspire. It wasn't important enough that everyone understood their tasks; they also needed to believe in them. That belief is the only thing that can direct the passion that every developer has.

EA Chicago closed its doors in the fall of 2007. *Lesson 5: The industry is volatile so be open to relocation. If you are, doors will always be open to you and networking will happen automatically.*

EA Redwood Shores

The closing of a studio is always painful, but the amazing HR staff at EA Chicago opened up a job fair at the studio during its final days. Studios all across EA and companies across the industry showed up to recruit the incredible talent of EA

Chicago. I remember talking to many studios, but I ended up going with an internal transfer to EA Redwood Shores in the San Francisco Bay Area. The game was *Dead Space.*

EA Tiburon had game dev down to a science, EA Chicago was all heart, but the *Dead Space* dev team had the work down to an artform. I started in January of 2008 as an Assistant Producer II and was put in charge of the UI (User Interface) team. In this industry, UI is an overlay on the game that offers secondary interactions or relays information so players can better understand what's going on. But on the *Dead Space* team, the UI was an experience. With the goal of never breaking the fourth wall, the User Interface was a system of holograms that existed in gameplay space as part of the fantasy. Most of this innovation was determined before I got there, but I had the honor of building and managing the team that would ship it.

The biggest differentiator for the Dead Space team was its culture. The team had amazing leaders. You didn't want to let them down. You didn't want to let anyone down. You put in 110 percent because everyone was putting in 110 percent. *Lesson 6: Attitude reflects leadership. If you see a poor work ethic across your studio, the instigator is usually at the top.*

Everyone on *Dead Space* felt like they had a responsibility to the game and its design. Great leadership facilitated that. One example, named the "$2 idea," came late in development when the leads noticed there weren't enough horror moments in the game. The leads called for everyone on the team to play the game and submit exciting horror ideas that were extremely cheap to implement. *Lesson 7: Every team is filled with passionate and amazing idea generators. Use them or lose them.*

Dead Space was highly praised for its innovations and quality. Many people across the team received promotions. I moved up to Associate Producer and made the move to *Dead Space 2* Multiplayer. But this time I was focused purely on game design.

I worked on *Dead Space 2* MP for a little over a year before an annual layoff wave went through the studio. I drew the short straw. That last day was a blur. A lot of coworkers expressed their surprise at my hard luck. I was surprised too, but I knew I would be alright. The EA Chicago shutdown had prepared me for this moment. It was time for the next adventure. *Lesson 8: Layoffs are a numbers game. You shouldn't dwell on it. As long as your colleagues know you have the skills and work hard, then your networking circle will be there for you.*

After taking a short break I decided to start interviewing again. I wanted to stay in the industry and ended up with two offers. One was for a production role at Lucas Arts in San Francisco and the other was for a Senior Multiplayer Designer position in New York City. I felt it was finally time to officially become a game designer and what better place to do it than NYC?

KAOS Studios (THQ)

I joined KAOS Studios in March of 2010 as the Senior Multiplayer Designer for the UI team on *Homefront*. Per usual, the UI team had been suffering from death by a thousand requests. As requests kept rolling in from the other teams at the studio, UI was expected to keep adding more pieces to their systems. Because of this, nothing felt cohesive, and the requests kept stacking. In these situations, the best thing to do is become a shield for your team: Give them time to pick up the pieces, prioritize all requirements, cut unnecessary items, and rebuild with a structured vision. The strategy went well and we got our heads above the water.

A lot of the UI requests were tied to our competitive game modes. One of our main modes, Battle Commander, was unproven, and the UI team felt the brunt of it. Every playtest triggered requests for more UI solutions. *Maybe the player doesn't understand. Maybe they aren't seeing this mission. The mode doesn't work because the UI isn't loud enough.* Sometimes the mode doesn't work because the game design doesn't work. It was my turn to bring a new perspective. *Lesson 10: If something isn't working, it's on you to (a) follow up and make sure someone is on it or (b) own it yourself. Take the initiative. Ignoring problems or expecting that someone else will handle them leads to crap games.*

Battle Commander was originally a mode of modes. The game would spawn new situations during the match and the AI Battle Commander would present you with side missions. These missions could include High Value Target, Supply Drop, or Capture Point. But players didn't seem to care about the side missions because they weren't directly tied to the win condition and felt like a distraction. No amount of UI can overcome the player's will. I worked with the engineers, and we pitched for Battle Commander to lean into the player's resolve instead of fighting it. This led us to double down on the only mission that was working, High Value Target. The new pitch became *Killstreaks earn you passive buffs and mark you as a High Value Target for the other team.* It was simple and it escalated. Players saw becoming a High Value Target as a badge of honor, an increased challenge, and a cool reward. Battle Commander had become a success. *Lesson 11: Always follow the fun. Don't try to outdesign it.*

KAOS Studios closed its doors in the summer of 2011, and THQ, its parent company, soon fell alongside it. The volatility of the industry showed itself again. Luckily, I was quickly recruited by Ubisoft and moved to Canada.

Ubisoft Toronto

Based on the industry hubs, I always assumed my next stop after NYC would be Los Angeles or Montreal, Quebec. I was surprised to hear Ubisoft had recently opened a studio in Toronto that was heading up the next *Splinter Cell*. I played through the previous iteration *(Splinter Cell: Conviction)*, interviewed, and secured a position as their Lead Game Designer for the Co-op Campaign.

My first semiofficial day with the studio was the summer BBQ on August 20, 2011. It turned out to be a relaxing Saturday on Centre Island just near downtown Toronto with the studio's employees and their families. We ate good food, played volleyball, and socialized over drinks. That solidified what I already noticed during my onsite interview, that this studio treated game development as a lifestyle. Never before had I felt so at home.

During my second week at the studio, the Co-op Campaign was cut due to scope concerns. Well, that was quick. I knew what would happen next. The same thing that happened at every other studio I worked at. And then it didn't happen. Nobody was let go. Everyone was shifted to other sections of the team. I shifted to a smaller co-op mandate and online systems. In my ten years at Ubisoft I never saw a large layoff at the studio. In that time, Ubisoft Toronto grew from 150 to more than 900 employees. *Lesson 12: The most important thing about a studio is its employees. Hire the right ones and never let them go.*

The co-op team fought hard to keep four smaller cooperative modes in *Splinter Cell: Blacklist*. One was a small story campaign, and the remaining three each tied to a specific playstyle that the game promoted. They were successful additions and something we were all proud of. After *Blacklist* shipped, I was part of two amazing teams whose games were put on hold. Around this time, I started focusing on the industry as a whole and the values I appreciated in game designers. This drove me to become a speaker at the Game Developers Conference (GDC).

In November of 2015, I joined the *Starlink: Battle for Atlas* team and soon after became its Game Director. There's something that attracts me to developing new franchises, but this time I made the decision based on the team rather than the project. The project itself was an enigma. The team had figured out many aspects of the game but didn't really know what the game was. They had hundreds of cool ideas but no Game Loop to bring them together. My first stop wasn't to talk to directors but to engage with the team. I pulled a lot of developers into one-on-one meetings and got their take on the real issues the team was facing. From here we worked together on solutions. *Lesson 13: Your biggest successes in game design will come from listening. By listening you can understand the real problems that need to be solved and push the team's ideas into systems that work.*

In March of 2020, I accepted the position of Game Design & UX Community Director with the goal of developing a stronger design culture at the studio. By then I had given three GDC talks on related topics and was excited to dive deeper into what game designers and UX designers would become at Ubisoft Toronto. I also remained a Game Director on a project. It would be tough juggling both jobs, but I knew that once I stepped away from development I would lose credibility with each passing day.

It's hard to summarize ten years of employment and all the knowledge gained in this time. Great leaders and passionate developers shaped that studio into what it is today, and they've all had a profound impact on my career and, therefore, the contents of this book.

In April of 2021, I decided to step away from Ubisoft Toronto.

Sledgehammer Games Toronto

At one point in 2021, an old colleague and friend hit me up about an opportunity to start a new Sledgehammer studio location in Toronto. To reiterate, a colleague I worked with at Ubisoft Toronto back in 2013 on *Splinter Cell Blacklist* asked me to join a studio filled with Dead Space devs I worked with back in 2008. I was in. I am in. We're currently ramping up and I couldn't be more excited. In May of 2021, I became a Creative Director and Employee #1 at Sledgehammer Games Toronto.

This Book

Each studio I was a part of worked differently. Each held different ideals and priorities. Each had different strengths and weaknesses that led to different successes and failures. But what was similar among all of them was the abundance of skills that each team had and the passion each developer shared to make something great.

As I advanced in my career, I not only became a student of games and game design but also of teams and their passion. I studied the people who made the games as much as I did the games themselves. I pondered the importance of inspiration above all else. A skilled team with a solid design can deliver a quality product. But an inspired team can break barriers and tear down mountains. An inspired team can create innovations that change the industry. And from that realization came one of the most important: Game designers are leaders. Even the most junior designer who owns only one feature must lead. That designer must inspire the team to drive that feature to be the best it can be. My study of game designers is what led to this book.

Some really solid books tackle the topic of game design, but few tackle my favorite topic, game designers. This book explores how game designers are more than just the people who employ game design. Our industry is still young and the role of game designers is still being determined. Studios across the industry have different expectations and mandates for this role. And after working at six AAA studios and four major publishers, I've developed a more complete definition of the game designer role, the skills it requires, and the expectations the team should have for it.

In the end, this book is just the start of the conversation. So please feel free to hit me up on Twitter (@Carrillo_GD) or on LinkedIn. If you do wish to connect, please do so by continuing the conversation and letting me know what you agreed with or disagreed with in this book. Hope to hear from you soon.

-Richard Carrillo

http://www.gamedesignerhandbook.com

PART ONE

●

DEFINITIONS

CHAPTER 1

DEFINING *GAME*

Any book about game design must first define what a game is—designers need to understand what they're actually designing. A book about game designers is no different. To truly define what a game is we must do a deep dive into what we know about games, starting with their structure. As you break down games into their structure, you'll notice that the simplest games you played during recess have a lot in common with the most complex games you play on your consoles.

To start, every game has three phases: setup, play, and finish. The last phase may become a source of disagreement, but let's start from the beginning.

The Setup Phase

The setup phase handles the starting point for all players, and altering it can become the easiest way to alter the game. For example, imagine starting *Monopoly* (Parker Brothers, 1935) with only $50. That's $1450 less than the original design in the rulebook. This is a simple and small change that will alter the game in a major way. Starting with only $50 drastically reduces the speed of the game and makes chance cards a nightmare that could knock you out in the first few minutes. The general goal for the setup is to start the game fair and balanced with the best chance of ramping into the play phase quickly. The setup phase ends when all players know the basic rules, understand their main goal, and are ready to play.

The Play Phase

The play phase is the meat of the experience and where the fun happens (hopefully). In this phase, players learn and employ the mechanics they'll be using to reach the finish phase. Altering the play phase can be difficult as one alteration can domino into changes for many other mechanics and systems.

For example, let's continue the earlier discussion on *Monopoly*. What if each player starts with $200 but all properties are owned by the bank and require rent or purchase whenever a player lands on one? The goal of this game is to work together with all other players to take down the bank. We'll call it *Breaking the Bank instead of Anti-Capitalistic Revolution* to keep it more lighthearted and American. Before you look for your old *Monopoly* board to try out this new game mode, let's stop and think of all the systems I just broke in the play phase:

- If this is a co-op game, what happens when other players land on your property?

- Is there no longer a reason to own all properties of the same color or all four railroads?

- What's the point of building houses or hotels? How does that hurt the bank?
- Does the bank lose when it runs out of money? How is that possible when it's gaining money on every purchase and only technically loses money when players "Pass Go"?
- What happens when the bank runs out of properties? Is that a victory for the players?

Very few of the mechanics and systems from *Monopoly* make sense in this new approach. Many of these mechanics need to be redesigned to fit the new game or cut altogether. And here lies one of the biggest messages in this book: Chasing cool ideas can break everything else you've been working on. It's on the game designer to look past the novelty of an idea and deep into the systems to see what breaks and how to fix it.

The Finish Phase

The finish phase is quite simply the end of the game when winners and losers are decided. You may disagree with this definition and think, for example, that more open-ended titles like *Minecraft* (Mojang, 2011) don't have a finish phase. But our fundamental disagreement isn't about whether *Minecraft* has a finish phase. The disagreement lies in defining what a game is. *Minecraft, Red Dead, Roblox* aren't individual games. These are deep worlds that house a collection of games. The finish phase has nothing to do with when the story ends or when you stop playing in these worlds. It has to do with the completion of the player's main goal through our second structural component: gameplay loops.

Gameplay Loops

Gameplay loops exist in the play phase and are the series of major actions the player takes to play the experience. Each gameplay loop is based on an Objective > Challenge > Reward structure that drives player motivation to progress through the loop.

```
        OBJECTIVE
       ↗         ↘
  REWARD  ←  CHALLENGE
```

- The **objective** is determined in the first beat and is what the player is trying to accomplish in order to progress the game or enter the finish phase.
- The **challenge** is primarily found in the second beat and is what the player must overcome to complete the objective.
- And the **reward**, the third beat, is what the player receives or avoids (including avoidance of a repercussion) after completing the objective.

A successful gameplay loop will offer a reward in the third beat that feeds back into the first beat of the loop in order to maintain player engagement. Modern games are filled with multiple gameplay loops that players will bounce between.

The *core* gameplay loop is the loop the player spends a majority of their time in to progress the game. This, therefore, is the loop that the devs should spend a majority of their time polishing. Here's an example core gameplay loop from *Tom Clancy's Splinter Cell: Blacklist* (Ubisoft, 2013), which treats every room of enemies as its own play phase:

```
        PLAN
   ↗         ↘
VANISH      EXECUTE
        ↵
```

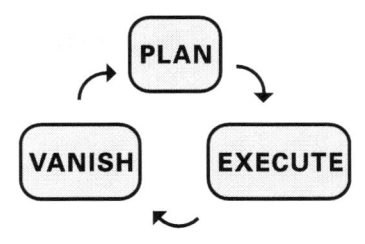

In *Splinter Cell*, when the player approaches a group of enemies, the core gameplay loop begins.

- **Plan**: Almost every encounter starts with the enemy unaware of the player's location. This gives the player an opportunity to study the encounter and plan an approach. This plan becomes the player's objective.

- **Execute**: The player enters the execute beat when ready to enact the plan. Executing the plan is the main challenge of the encounter.

- **Vanish**: A successful execution will advance the player past the encounter and back into a stealth state. The reward is both the advancement and the return to stealth. All of this allows the player to continue to the next set of unaware enemies.

The Plan > Execute > Vanish loop is how the player progresses through each mission in *Splinter Cell*. Complex games like this contain many other gameplay loops. The full collection of loops that makes up the entire playable experience is called the game loop.

The purpose to identifying your loops is to focus your effort as you develop features. The team should focus on adding depth to the core gameplay loop before adding other gameplay loops onto the experience.

Example Games & Loops

In this section we'll go through a few example games and break down their structures into phases and loops.

Rock, Paper, Scissors **(RPS)**

RPS is one of the simplest and most pure games out there.

Setup. Two players each with at least one hand. The goal is to beat the other player in a game of chance.

Play. One Gameplay Loop: Plan > Throw > Resolve.

- **Plan:** The objective is to beat your opponent by choosing the correct option. Winning is as much about making your choice as it is predicting what your opponent will choose.

- **Throw:** Pick from one of three options. Your choice must be revealed at the same time as your opponent. Each option has an equal chance to win, lose, or draw.

- **Resolve:** Complete humiliation for the player who chose the incorrect option.

Finish. Winner takes all or best two out of three. RPS is usually not played for fun but used to determine who gets the last of something (like a slice of pizza) or who has to do a task nobody wants to do (like take out the trash).

Game Loop & Gameplay Loop:

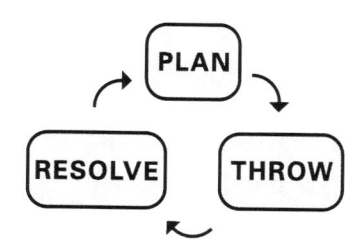

Defining *Game*

Analysis. RPS is considered the Holy Grail of game design as its core three-option system is referenced by countless games in the industry. With its simple setup, single gameplay loop, and perfect balance, it's no wonder this game has lasted centuries.

Even though RPS seems like a game of chance, it actually has a competitive following. In competitive play it's seen as a game of patterns. In a best two out of three setting, the first option may be random, but where the game goes from there is layered in strategies based in psychology. If you won with Scissors, you may feel inclined to try it again. If you lose to Rock, you may go Paper next. It becomes a game of understanding your opponent and trying to outsmart them. So next time you play, just know that the most common sign thrown is Rock.

Tag

Tag is generally the go-to game for groups of kids due to its simplicity in setup and play and its ability to get participants to expend a massive amount of energy. Is basketball a better game? Yes. Do I have a basketball, hoop, and court available? No.

Setup. At least three players and an area to chase each other in. The goal is to not be It. If you are It, tag an opponent to transfer the It state.

Play. Two gameplay loops.

It Loop: Target > Chase > Tag

- **Target:** Targeting an opponent sets your objective. The opponent may be the closest person or one you know you can catch.
- **Chase:** The challenge is getting in range of a tag. Chase after your target until you are able to touch them.

- **Tag:** You are rewarded by no longer being It.

Not It Loop: Identify > Flee > Dodge

- **Identify:** Understanding who is It and spotting them sets your objective. You must refrain from being tagged.
- **Flee:** The challenge is staying out of arms reach from the player deemed It but also staying close enough to the action to understand who is It.
- **Dodge:** Your reward is remaining not It and therefore remaining superior to all others who have been It.

Finish. "Time for dinner!" Tag generally times out with the last player being It deemed the loser. The true winner is generally someone who was never tagged or spent the least time being It.

Game Loop & Gameplay Loops:

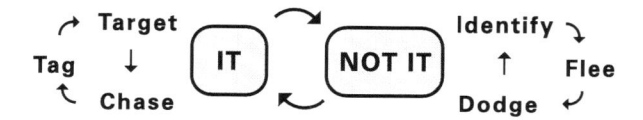

```
      ↗ Target                    Identify ↘
  Tag  ↓      IT  ⇄  NOT IT    ↑         Flee
      ↖ Chase                    Dodge   ↙
```

Analysis. Although *Tag* has a second gameplay loop, it is much simpler than RPS in its challenge systems. It's so simple that the kids playing it will generally solve its core problems with layers of design. "No tag-backs" may be the first true game design that children understand. Kids understand that it's too easy to touch someone who put themselves in range to touch you, and so with "tag-backs" the game can quickly devolve into a contest between solely two people.

Another game design lesson exists within the game of *Tag*. A seasoned game designer may look at the systems and determine that once the "slow kid" is It, the game is over. Maybe the kid who is It should always have a speed boost? But during actual play something amazing happens. If the player who is It is having trouble tagging someone, other players will alter their gameplay loop with a new objective to get as close as they can to the It player without being tagged. The lesson: Paper design can be great to get started but nothing beats watching players play your experience. You will learn a lot more that way about the positives and negatives of your design.

Minecraft

A designer could write an entire book analyzing the gameplay loops of *Minecraft*. For this specific example, I'll try to summarize just a few of the gameplay loops to get my point across.

Setup. You need a PC/console/mobile device, an installed *Minecraft* game, a valid input device, a front end flow leading to your avatar standing in the world ready to mine and/or craft, and a basic understanding of controls. Although many people may say that the setup phase isn't part of the game, I still believe it to be a very important part of the user experience and one of the biggest blockers for people to play. Understanding and lessening your setup will allow more players to share your experience.

The goal, in this example, is to craft the tool/weapon/armor/equipment you've been lacking.

Play. The game includes many gameplay loops including Explore/Mine/Craft/Build/Battle. These loops come together around player-determined objectives and finish requirements.

Explore Loop: Target > Nav > Survey

- **Target**: Minecraft worlds are large and contain vast areas to explore. The player sets the objective by determining an area or direction to explore further, possibly for knowledge, materials, or adventure.

- **Nav:** Reaching your desired area is the challenge. Climb, dig, swim, and possibly run into combat along the way.
- **Survey:** As you map out the world, your reward is knowledge, materials, and adventure. The farther you go on your journey, the more exciting things you'll find.

Mine Loop: Locate > Mine > Collect

- **Locate:** Locating a mineral you want sets your objective.
- **Mine:** Mining is a very simple task but can be somewhat of a challenge when your pick can't reach the blocks. Position yourself correctly and mine as efficiently as possible. Craft better picks to ease your task.
- **Collect:** Your reward is the minerals you've collected and usually some bonus minerals you didn't expect to find along the way.

Craft Loop: Plan > Set > Complete

- **Plan:** Determining what you want to craft sets your objective. You're generally compelled by your tools breaking, your wish to survive longer, or your desire to explore further.
- **Set:** Setting an object to be crafted requires you to have all the required materials. This drives you into the explore loop to search for the material. Once set, crafting may take time.
- **Complete:** Your reward is the crafted object. This can be used, placed, or equipped to advance your experience.

Finish. The loop is finished when your crafting is complete. As you progress through the game, you'll find that powerful items require rare materials, which, can be more easily acquired by using other powerful items. All gameplay loops drive you into others.

Core Gameplay Loop:

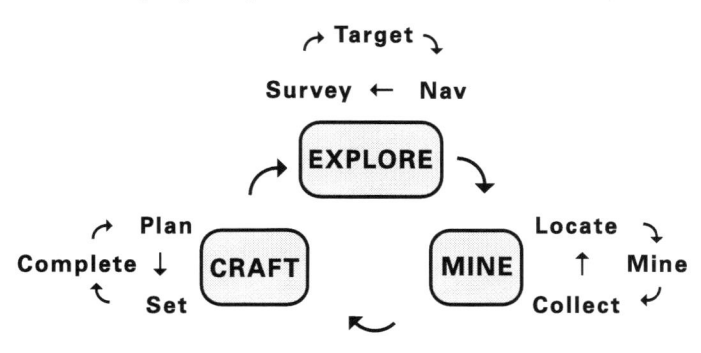

```
              ↗ Target ↘
          Survey ← Nav
           ↗ [EXPLORE] ↘
    ↗ Plan              Locate ↘
Complete ↓ [CRAFT]   [MINE] ↑ Mine
    ↖ Set              Collect ↙
              ↖
```

Analysis. *Minecraft's* open exploration, crafting, and building systems give the feeling of "infinite" player-driven goals. However, in any game, if players aren't feeling challenged or don't feel like they are increasing their skills, they'll stop playing. Thus, the goals players create for themselves will generally increase in challenge and complexity each and every time. Therefore, games with player-driven goals should keep the boundaries of their systems large enough to give a feeling of endless exploration, depth, and complexity. *Minecraft* does this well with tons of depth in every system.

As mentioned, *Minecraft* has many gameplay loops that link to each other in a variety of ways. Designing your gameplay loops to have deep interactions with one another allows you to support multiple loops while reusing the same systems and mechanics. For example, if the player's goal was to build a structure, they'd Explore > Mine > Build. If it was to complete an armor set, they'd Explore > Mine > Craft. If it was to clear out a large dungeon, they'd Explore > Battle > Mine. Depth in your systems means your gameplay loops can have a lot of interactions, allowing the player to move through them with great purpose.

Finally, rearranging existing gameplay loops is a great way to brainstorm new experiences. For example, what would it mean to Battle > Craft > Mine? It could mean that certain enemies drop recipes and materials that are crafted into a map to an undiscovered location or crafted into a key that unlocks a vault. Both could house amazing rare mineral deposits. This type of brainstorming can lead to unique ideas that reuse a lot of developed systems. This is the strength of identifying and understanding your gameplay loops.

Finalizing the Definition

What we've discussed so far are the high-level structural components of a game. The low-level components are all the rules, mechanics, and systems that make each game unique. These are the bulk of what game designers design, and we'll talk more about them in the next chapter. For now, let's finalize our definition of *game*.

> **Game:** A form of play with external forces or setups <u>designed</u> to keep players from achieving their goal, which can be overcome through skill or chance.

The key word in this definition is <u>designed</u> (that's why I underlined it). Every game in the history of the world was designed by someone. They designed the rules of play and designed the forces in opposition. Sometimes that opposition is other players, sometimes it's AI, and sometimes it's simply a puzzle or timer. If there isn't something opposing you from achieving your goal then you aren't playing a game.

Let's look at a counter example to this definition. Imagine you're stuck in morning traffic and you have twelve minutes to get to work or you'll be late. Is this a game? No—this is a task with a time limit. But what if I, as the designer, added spaces in between the cars and stuck a twelve-minute timer on your dashboard? Is this a game? Closer. The last missing piece is found in the term "play." In this example the driver would be the player. But to play you need to know you are a player. So, if you are a driver stuck in morning traffic that you've been told is designed for you to beat with a twelve-minute timer on your dash, then yes, this is a game.

After determining the *game* definition, a philosophical question hit me as I stared at the "can be overcome" condition. Does a game need to be winnable? Can the whole experience be rigged and still be considered a game? Carnival games quickly come to mind. From tossing rings onto bottles to rolling bowling balls on rails, there is something unbelievably fun about playing a quick game of skill/chance for a prize that you don't really want to have in your house. And after seeing the employee hose down the playing field with a can of grease, I concluded that rigging the experience doesn't stop it from being considered a game. In fact, most players see this rigging as an extra challenge or evidence that it requires some luck to win.

So games can be rigged but how rigged? What if the player has no chance of winning? For that discussion let's turn to the example of *Three-Card Monte* (a.k.a. Find the Queen).

Three-Card Monte

Setup. A dealer sets three cards face down on a table. The dealer reveals the red queen as one of the cards and returns it to the face-down position. The goal is to identify the red queen card after the dealer shuffles the cards.

Play. One gameplay loop: Identify > Track > Select

- **Identify:** Once you're shown the queen, your objective is never to lose it.

- **Track:** The dealer shuffles the cards around the table in front of the player's eyes. The cards are moved fast, over and under each other. Once the shuffle has ended, there are three face-down cards for the player to choose from.
- **Select:** You beat the dealer and might win money.

Finish. After one easy round of winning, you may keep playing. And then you'll keep losing.

Analysis. Everyone has seen this game played in movies and on TV shows on the streets of New York. The dealer will generally allow a player to win once and, from that moment on, the dealer palms the queen so the player can never win again. The player (on TV at least) fully believes they are playing a fair game and will continue playing until they've lost all their money. Is this a game? The player believes it is. So is it a game as long as the player believes they can win?

If I were to play LeBron James in a game of one-on-one basketball I know I would have zero chance of even scoring, but that basketball match would still be considered a game. When is a game no longer a game? Let's say we make the rim of the hoop so small the ball can't even fit. Now it's finally rigged in a way that makes it not a game. A game does not need to be winnable but it must be playable; once its gameplay loops are broken then it can't be played. Making it impossible for the ball to go through the hoop in a game of basketball breaks the gameplay loops, and now everybody is upset and nobody is playing a game. In short, a game always needs to be able to enter the finish phase even if *you* won't be declared the victor when you get there.

Earlier I discussed the example in *Tag* where the slow player being "It" should theoretically ruin the game. But in many cases where you expect things to fail, players will alter your loops to allow for success. Sometimes, players who know the cheat will adjust the game to overcome it. The *Three-card Monte* player will start to play a new game of "Find the Palmed Queen." The person playing against LeBron will set a personal goal of making one shot. If you're playing *Rock, Paper, Scissors* against a mind reader, you will lose every match. But once you're informed about your opponent, you will try to beat the system by thinking of one option but throwing another.

As a game designer, you must watch players interact with your experience. Doing so will reveal more about your gameplay loops than your paper designs showcased. Players will always test the loops, optimize them, try to break them, or see if they can bypass them. If you give them an almost impossible task, they may surprise you in what they do. Those surprises can lead to new discoveries for you and new loops for your game.

Metagame

The definition of metagame is so widely different from studio to studio that I was specifically asked to cover it in this book (someone just metagamed my book!). Some studios think of the metagame as progression systems that sit on top of the core gameplay loops. Others liken it to min/maxing their progression or understanding the optimal strategy (the meta).

The actual metagame exists outside the game loop altogether. It's a layer of strategy in which players are considered to be gaming the entire experience. The easiest example is in the *Rock, Paper, Scissors* competitive scene I mentioned earlier. The game itself is a game of chance. But playing the psychology of your opponent is entering a second game that sits above the first. Another example would be reading your opponent's hand gesture mid-throw and altering yours in response. You would then be playing outside the rules and loops of the game and thus have created a metagame that sits above it.

> **Metagame:** A strategy layer, that sits outside of a game's game loop, in which the player bases decisions on outside knowledge or previous round knowledge.

My best advice is to worry about your game loop and gameplay loops first. Make sure those are solid and testing well before you concern yourself with the metagame.

Modern Games

I've defined what a game is but making one doesn't mean it will succeed in today's market. If you make another *Rock, Paper, Scissors or Tag*, I highly doubt you'll be able grab the public's attention enough to call it a winner (gauntlet thrown if you'd like to make the attempt).

So what makes a game modern? Deep strategy? Community? Player freedom and self-expression? In my experience, there is no single answer. Developing a modern game is generally about building on top of current market trends or pulling from trends that exist outside of our industry. But every now and then an innovation also comes out of nowhere and flips the industry on its head.

The market is huge with billions of players all looking for an experience they can lose themselves in. A modern game is really anything you want it to be, just like modern art. The only thing needed to make a modern game is a modern game designer. That's you!!! Do you feel all warm and fuzzy?

CHAPTER 2

DEFINING *GAME DESIGN*

If you've researched games before, you've probably seen many game definitions from other designers, theorists, and enthusiasts. Most are academic approaches that can lead to great debates while others can leave you confused. I always prefer a practical approach to everything I do. In this case that means creating a practical definition that can be used as a beacon to determine what game design requires from game designers. As a reminder, here is the *game* definition I gave in Chapter 1:

> **Game:** A form of play with external forces or setups <u>designed</u> to keep players from achieving their goal, which can be overcome through skill or chance.

Based on this definition, the entire purpose of game design is to create challenge and opposition for the player. This may seem too simple, so let's look at an example. What if I ask you to throw a tennis ball against the wall? You're probably thinking, "Why? That sounds boring." Okay, what if I ask you to take a pencil, mark a dot on the wall, and then throw the tennis ball and hit that dot three times in a row without missing? I bet something inside you just stirred. An excitement. A feeling that you know this will be a challenge but you're pretty sure you can do it. Now what if I also add that I completed that same challenge after twenty-two throws, and I bet you can't beat it. "Damnit, where's my tennis ball?!?"

Tennis Wall

Setup. A tennis ball, a wall, and a marked spot on the wall that is your target. The player must have a way to toss the ball and retrieve it. The goal is to hit the marked spot on the wall with the tennis ball three times in a row without missing.

Play. One Loop: Aim > Throw > Retrieve

- **Aim:** Your objective is to hit the marked dot on the wall with the tennis ball.

- **Throw:** Your challenge is achieving the precision it takes to hit the dot with the ball.

- **Retrieve:** Catch or chase after the ball. Hitting the dot means you've progressed another one-third of the way toward your goal, as long as you don't miss the next throw.

Finish. You hit the dot three times in a row and completed the task. But did you do it in under twenty-two total throws? If not, hahahahahaha! If so, whatever. It's just a stupid game.

Some of you will attempt to win this game by standing an inch away from the wall. You'll feel pretty smart about yourself because I didn't specify a distance requirement. Why didn't I? I must be a bad designer or maybe you're an amazing gamer. The designer's constant struggle is to create the perfect challenge that players feel equipped to tackle but will still prove to be challenging. This means creating rules that ensure a player can't cheat the challenge or, if they can, that the designer intended that outcome to be an option.

Rules

Rules are simply about governing player action. But more complexly, rules are the basic building blocks of everything in the game. Rules are established in the setup phase.

Tennis Wall seems like it needs very few rules, just the requirements listed in the setup phase. I could add another one that requires the player to be a minimum of 10 feet from the wall before throwing and another about how small the pencil mark needs to be. But those are all the rules we'd need, right?

In reality, *Tennis Wall* actually has many more rules. We just don't usually think about them because we've dealt with these rules—physics—since birth. These include the fact that the ball is affected by gravity, that it can't go through the wall, and that it bounces. Overcoming physics with precision is essentially the main challenge of the game. And since this game exists in the real world, the game design can take these rules for granted. But if this game existed in a virtual world, the design would require more effort to create the rules of physics for that world. In video games, game design must first determine the rules for how the world works before challenges can be created within that world for the player to overcome.

When designing a virtual world's rules, you can start by asking these questions:

- What are the boundaries of the world?
- What are the boundaries of the player in this world?
- What is the gravitational pull in this world? Which way does it pull? Is it the same for the player and for the ball?
- Is the player's avatar driven through animation, physics, or both? What happens when the player walks into the wall?

- Is there collision with the wall? Is it dynamic (can be moved) or static (can never be moved)? What about the ball?
- What is the level of bounciness and friction on these collisions?

All of these questions and many more must be answered before the meat of the game can be defined. In video games, the creation of rules first means the creation of the world. Once you've figured out the world, then you can turn to the actions, or mechanics, the player can perform in it.

Mechanics

A mechanic is anything the player uses to interact with the game or that the game uses to interact with itself or the player. Mechanics have input (from the player or another source) and output (from the game). Mechanics exist in the play phase.

Tennis Wall has two main player mechanics. One mechanic is throwing the ball and the other is catching it. The creation of the dot on the wall is technically not a mechanic since it doesn't exist in the play phase. Instead, it is the player's creation of the goal. Throwing the ball or catching it takes input from the player and progresses the main gameplay loop. Of course, if you don't catch the ball and it bounces away, you need a navigation mechanic to chase it down. If the ball rolls under a table, you'll need a crouch mechanic to go after it. God forbid it flies out the window and bounces across the street. Let's just call that Game Over. The more possible challenges your game supports, the more mechanics you'll want to create to give the player opportunities to overcome those challenges (or vice-versa). This is one of the many reasons games can quickly become overscoped.

Mechanics can also be controlled by the game instead of the player, although *Tennis Wall* doesn't utilize any such mechanics. These types of mechanics are harder to produce in the real world as they need some sort of intelligent or designed opposition to control them (i.e., artificial intelligence, AI). Here are a couple of possible examples of these types of mechanics for *Tennis Wall:*

- **Real World.** You train your dog to try to retrieve the ball before the player can. Once the ball is retrieved, the dog tries to hide it somewhere in the house. This creates the mechanics dog retrieve, dog navigate, and dog hide ball. Furthermore, this creates a dog gameplay loop, and now the player needs mechanics to counter the dog.

- **Virtual World.** Laser turrets are placed around the goal to damage and kill you before you're able to score (now the player's avatar needs hit points, damage effects, and a death state). The turrets track the ball and shoot whoever is holding it after a one-second delay. This creates the mechanics track and fire for the turrets.

When designing intelligent opposition, it's beneficial for the AI (or Dog Intelligence in the real-world example) to receive its own gameplay loop. This gives the AI more depth and purpose in the game rather than one-off challenges.

Gameplay Breadth & Depth

When discussing gameplay breadth and depth, we're really discussing mechanics. Gameplay breadth refers to the many individual mechanics that have unique interactions with the world and unique reactions from the world. An example of this is the sheer volume of things you can do in *Grand Theft Auto V* (Rockstar Games, 2013). On top of all the expected mechanics, you can even play a game of tennis. These mechanics may add richness to the world and to new gameplay loops, but they add little depth to the original loops. Gameplay breadth can lead to toy box experiences in which the player wants to try out all the different mechanics available. It can be great as long as you have the scope to build it.

Gameplay *depth* refers to the mechanics that have deeper interactions with multiple systems. Depth allows for a maximum amount of output while generally keeping the amount of unique input to a smaller, more manageable scope. Depth also increases the importance of each individual mechanic as it gains more interactions with other systems. Nintendo games do a great job at building depth while minimizing scope. *Super Mario Bros.* (Nintendo, 1985), for example, offered a large experience with just a few simple player inputs and mechanics. More recently, the design team for *The Legend of Zelda: Breath of the Wild* (Nintendo, 2017) required that each new mechanic or feature have multiple interactions with other systems.[1] This decision prompted players to ensure they always had wooden weapons during a lightning storm as metal weapons would attract bolts of lightning. Gameplay depth leads to more unique, emergent experiences that push players to try individual mechanics in a wide range of scenarios.

Systems

Systems are how games interpolate a series of mechanics and rules. Systems determine how everything works together and interacts to create the gameplay experience. Systems exist in the play phase.

---

[1] Hidemaro Fujibayashi, *Breaking Conventions with The Legend of Zelda: Breath of the Wild,* Game Developers Conference, 2017

In *TennisWall*, the player throws the ball toward the wall, gravity pulls it down, the wall exerts a force that bounces the ball off the wall, and finally the player attempts to catch or retrieve the ball. This is one system that ties together two mechanics (throw + retrieve) and the rules of the world. Systems are easier to understand when displayed via diagrams that showcase their concepts and connections. These diagrams are known as *conceptual models*. Here's one for *TennisWall*:

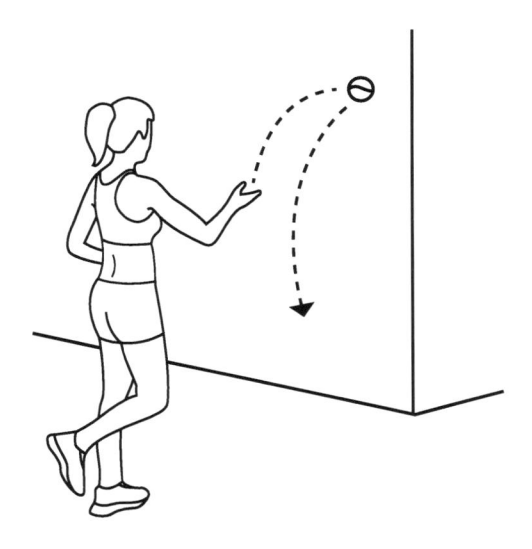

Another example is found in *Rock, Paper, Scissors*. RPS has three mechanics. Let's start with everyone's favorite, Rock. The player input consists of making a fist, which is generally the default hand position at the start of the game. I haven't decided if people who always throw Rock are lazy, are indecisive, or just love rocks. The output of throwing Rock is either tying against another Rock, beating Scissors, or losing to Paper. Here's the conceptual model for RPS to showcase its options and interactions:

The Role of a Great Game Designer

SCISSORS
beats paper

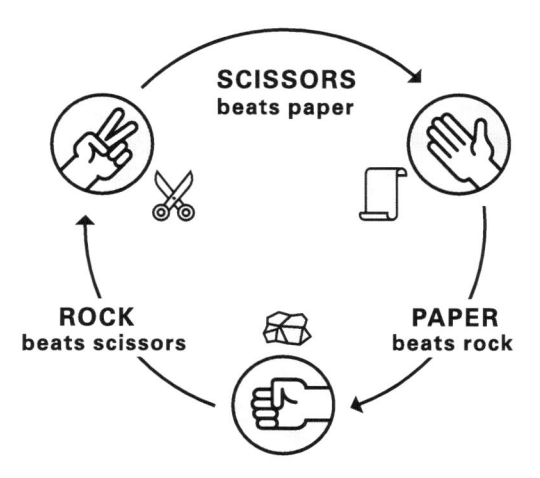

PAPER
beats rock

ROCK
beats scissors

The more complex your systems get, the more you'll want to draw them out to ensure balance. As you can see from the diagram, this three-option system is simple yet perfectly balanced.

What happens if we take away an option? What happens if we add an option? This is where game design shines. Whenever someone pitches to add or remove something from the game, the designer must always think in terms of mechanics and systems. How does one idea affect the entire experience? In RPS, take an option away and the whole thing falls apart. One option either always wins or it's always a draw. Add an option instead and it still breaks. Drawing out the conceptual model can help us understand why:

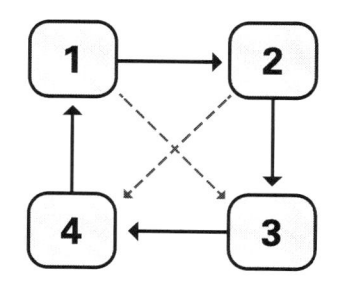

Defining *Game Design*

At the start, this four-option system feels like it might work as each option beats the one that comes after it. But when you start to question how 1 and 3 interact or 2 and 4, you'll see that the system becomes unbalanced. Now options 1 and 2 are vastly superior as they can beat two options, but 3 and 4 can only beat one option and will lose to two. Game design is about maintaining systems and ensuring their success. RPS can only maintain balance by adding two options at a time. An example of this can be found in the five-option version called *Rock, Paper, Scissors, Lizard, Spock* (created by Sam Kass and Karen Bryla):

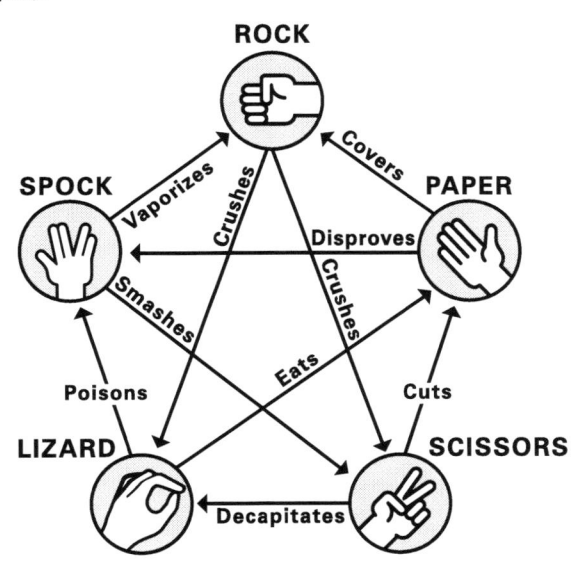

RPSLS has two problems. One is the fact that there are two Ss in its acronym (ugh, I hate it). But the more important issue is that it's difficult to recall the correct interactions among mechanics. Paper disproves Spock? What?

In game design there are two categories of systems, back-end and front-end. Back-end systems are behind the scenes and generally build the world. The player doesn't need to understand them. An example of back-end systems are the means by which an open-world game spawns enemies or creatures. Most of the time all the player cares about is that the world is populated, but there are deep systems maintaining when things spawn and why. Front-end systems, on the other hand, need to be fully understood and utilized by the player. How the options in RPS interact is an example of a front-end system. The player must fully comprehend how the system functions in order to play the game. This means maintaining a proper conceptual model in their mind of that system. Maintaining that conceptual model is more difficult with RPSLS but easier in games like *Pokémon* (Nintendo, 1996) that have many more options. Why would more options be easier to understand? There is one major reason why: fantasy.

Fantasy

A game's fantasy is the narrative world/theme that the experience exists in and to which all rules, mechanics, and systems contribute. To understand how fantasy is part of game design, we need to revisit our definition of the word *game*:

> **Game:** A form of play with external forces or setups <u>designed</u> to keep players from achieving their goal, which can be overcome through skill or chance.

Fantasy exists in our definition as "form of play." One of the earliest forms of play we learn as children is to pretend you are someone or something else: A knight storming a castle, a gunslinger in the Old West, a cop chasing down robbers. Make-believe is at the core of play and therefore an extremely important part of game design, not only to build an atmosphere that hooks players (although that's huge too) but also to help sell your systems and interactions. For example, there's a vampire in the next room and on the table you see a shotgun, a shovel, and a wooden stake. Which do you take? What if it was a zombie? A strong fantasy can help to build a solid and memorable conceptual model in each player's mind.

Let's turn back to Rock, Paper, Scissors and its fantasy. There are two:

1. Rock crushes Scissors, Paper covers Rock, Scissors cuts Paper.
2. Military destroys Technology, Diplomacy pacifies Military, Technology overcomes Diplomacy.

Although Option 2 builds a deeper, more meaningful fantasy, Option 1 is much easier to remember since it correlates directly to the hand gestures. Thus, Option 1 will almost always be the preferred fantasy. Now let's take another look at RPSLS:

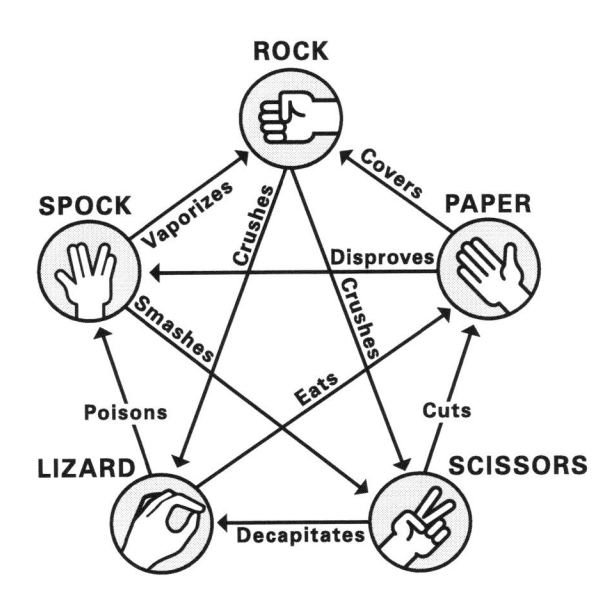

The original RPS fantasy focuses on how these specific objects could actually interact with each other. With that in mind, it's easy to understand how Lizard correlates to everything else. But once Spock enters the game, everything falls apart. Spock isn't just a Vulcan; he's a Vulcan with a phaser weapon, which wouldn't just vaporize rock but could vaporize everything. So why does he bother to smash Scissors? And now Lizard is suddenly poisonous? And Paper is no longer paper; it's suddenly a logical document, but only when dealing with the Spock option. The interactions become more complex as each option switches between fantasies. This makes it harder to remember the Spock interactions and to play. As a game designer, I'm bugged by these discrepancies, and I hope you are too. This five-option system has a significant problem that needs to be solved. Can you solve it?

For now, let's look at one of the more extreme references of RPS with *Pokémon*:

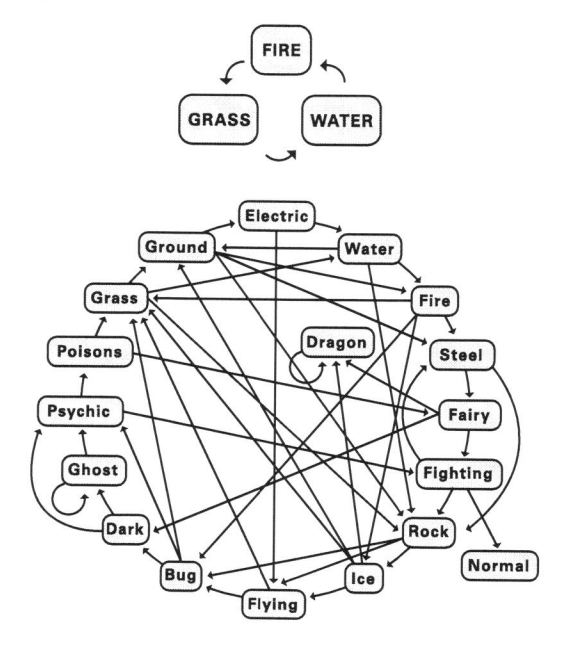

Defining *Game Design*

Fire beats Grass, Grass beats Water, and Water beats Fire. But as all types are entered into the system you'll see that Pokémon does not offer a balanced RPS system. Each type doesn't evenly win or lose. Normal type has almost no interaction except that it loses to Fighting. This system also has so many types that it's difficult to redraw the conceptual model from memory. But where this system shines is in the fact that it never breaks its fantasy. This makes it easier to learn. When thinking about two types battling, you can imagine the appropriate outcome within the fantasy.

Although fantasy is a useful tool to increase a game's marketability and capture a consumer base, it's also useful from a game design perspective in helping players build and memorize the conceptual models of a game's systems. Designers must never forget the importance of fantasy and play.

Our Definition of Game Design

By understanding and breaking down the definition of *game*, we've been able to gain a more practical view of game design as a whole, resulting in a definition of *game design:*

> **Game:** A form of play with external forces or setups <u>designed</u> to keep players from achieving their goal, which can be overcome through skill or chance.
> ↓
> **Game Design:** The art of designing play through fantasy and mechanics, while using rules and systems to create challenge in opposition of the player's goal in a game.

Most designers focus on an individual piece of the definition and move outward from there. For example, some designers may first focus on nailing down the fantasy and then they move on to mechanics. Others may focus on the world's rules and systems and then turn to how the player plays in that world. There is no wrong approach as long as you're working toward the whole.

The Player's Goal

If you look back at our game design definition, you'll notice there's one last piece we haven't talked about yet: the player's goal. This can refer to the player's objective in a gameplay loop or the finish goal of the entire game. In either case, the player's goal is about overcoming challenge. The definition says that rules and systems create the challenge, but there is no point for those rules and systems to exist if the player's goal doesn't drive them through those rules and systems.

The definition also doesn't specifically state where the player's goal comes from. That's because it can be design driven or player driven.

Design-driven goals are dictated by the game and therefore set the challenge. For a quick example we can turn to dungeon crawlers that lock you in a room with an enemy. The enemy has the key to open the door. The design-driven goal here is to defeat the enemy to unlock the door. One potential complication of design-driven goals is that they need to be appropriately challenging for all players, which can be difficult to accomplish since there's always a wide variety of skill levels in a player base. Games generally mitigate this problem by allowing the player to set the difficulty of the overall experience.

Player-driven goals are set by the player. For players to set their own appropriately challenging goals, the game must have systems that allow goals to be set (e.g., *Minecraft*) and a clear conceptual model so the player can understand the opportunities. Let's go back to our dungeon crawler example of the player being locked in a room with an enemy. To open this challenge up to be player driven, we would need to incorporate deeper systems and more opportunities for the player to create their own goal and to know that this is possible. Here are some options:

- The player can leave the way they came in. To continue the game, the player doesn't need to complete the dungeon.
- There are other pathways that lead to the room behind the locked door (vents, portals, etc.)
- The door can be opened in other ways or even destroyed.
- The door key can be acquired by theft or by bartering with the enemy.
- The enemy can be charmed to join the player's team.
- The player can purchase the dungeon—now they're rooting for the key-holding enemy.

Player-driven games are understandably more difficult to design, but if done right they can offer more replayability and retention in PvE experiences (Player versus Environment).

Whichever system is used, the player's goal drives the entire experience.

Fun

Another element of the player's goals is, presumably, to have fun. Throughout my career I've encountered plenty of designers who consider fun to be something subjective and immeasurable. Other designers consider it to be the true goal of good game design and what everything should be pushing toward. I side with the latter. Using our game design definition, we can detail a practical description of what fun means for games:

> Fun = Play + Challenge

This is an extremely simplified definition. One experience can have all play and no challenge: playing house as a kid or with a new action figure. Another can have all challenge and no play: working through a hard C++ problem. Exciting play can overcome low challenge and vice-versa.

This definition isn't practical enough, so we must dive deeper based on the tenets of game design:

> Fun = Play + Challenge
> ↓
> Fun = <u>Exciting</u> Fantasy/Mechanics + <u>Challenging</u> Goals/Systems

How do we define *exciting* in regards to fantasy or mechanics? Let's discuss some examples. Generally, a physics-based grappling hook is a more exciting mechanic than throwing a rock. But in the right context or with the right-sized rock, throwing a rock could be extremely exciting. If the grappling hook can attach to any surface and the player's character can swing or be pulled with physics, then the mechanic presents a wide variety of opportunities and instantly excites the mind. Excitement is a scale of reference that encompasses the novelty, context, or utility of the fantasy or mechanic in question. Exciting mechanics without challenging goals can lead to a sandbox experience that provides lots of toys to play with. With good enough mechanics, players will end up creating their own goals and just play.

What is the definition of *challenging* in regards to goals or systems? This one is simpler since *challenging* is more logic based than emotionally driven. Challenge is the degree of mental or physical exertion or finesse required to overcome an obstacle. In *Tennis Wall,* throwing the ball against the wall isn't an exciting mechanic (unless you're new to physics) but an appropriate challenge—like hitting a small target on the wall—can make the game fun. Offering challenging goals without exciting mechanics may mean that deeper strategies drive the fun or that the game is focused on pure Player versus Player (PvP) competition.

In the right type of game, a physics-based grappling hook can offer both excitement and challenge. Challenge here comes in the form of mastery or gaining competency. For many players, these types of physics-based mechanics may feel random at first, but as they learn the rules they'll begin to explore more difficult challenges. The topic of mastery always brings up the age-old question: Is it better to design for accessibility or mastery? The answer is BOTH! The question makes no sense as accessibility and mastery aren't at opposite ends of a spectrum.

And now for the final definition:

> **Fun (in games):** Engagement through the use of exciting fantasy and mechanics to overcome challenging systems and achieve one's goal.

When it comes to either excitement or challenge, the fun produced is never infinite. Exciting experiences will grow old over time as the novelty fades. Challenging experiences are only fun as long as the challenge remains. In the end it's in your best interest as a game designer to strive for both excitement *and* challenge. And trying to maintain both requires a balance between teaching new mechanics and increasing the challenge on learned mechanics. Throwing too many mechanics at the player early on leads to players never learning appropriately.

Throwing too difficult challenges early on leads to players being frustrated. But going too long without new mechanics or new challenges will lead to a stale experience. One of the tougher design jobs is fine-tuning the pace of learning and challenge.

Not all games need grappling hooks (surprising, right?). Sometimes the best way to create an innovative experience is to infuse excitement or challenge where the other exists or infuse both where neither exists. For example, opening a door in a game isn't in and of itself an exciting mechanic or a challenging system. But infusing excitement and challenge into opening doors might lead to a truly innovative and fun door game.

CHAPTER 3

ENTER THE GAME DESIGNER

Game design is a field or process. *Game designer* is a vocation. Game designers are a part of a development team. How they work with and fit within that team is as important as the game design itself. One person can function as an entire development team, but the moment you add a second developer is the moment you need to understand the game designer's roles and responsibilities that I lay out in this chapter.

As I mentioned before, game designers are leaders. They own the vision for what the game will become and must use it to inspire the team and drive the gameplay experience. All eyes are on them. More importantly, game designers must rouse the team's passion and drive that passion toward a successful design that meets the vision, integrates with all other systems, and can succeed in the current market.

The biggest misconception about the role comes from a misunderstanding of ownership and an unhealthy idea of control, often expressed in one or more of the following ways:

- "I will control the gameplay experience."
- "The team will work on *my* ideas."
- "I will create a game that everyone will love."

- "The ideas I've had for years will finally be formed into the experience of *my* dreams."

Unless you are working on a dev team of one, these statements couldn't be further from reality. The more people you work with, the more you'll understand how this misconception around *"my* ideas" and *"my* dreams" will lead you to failure rather than success. The simplest way to sum up the true job of the game designer is this:

> **Game designers** drive the gameplay experience by owning the gameplay vision and collaborating with the team on the design.

Designers lead the gameplay experience, but the only piece they really own is the vision:

> **Vision** is the understanding of how all the pieces will come together to create the experience.

Even the most junior game designers own the vision for how their systems will come together and integrate with the high-level vision laid out by the directors.

Here are some examples of team structure and ownership for the design family:

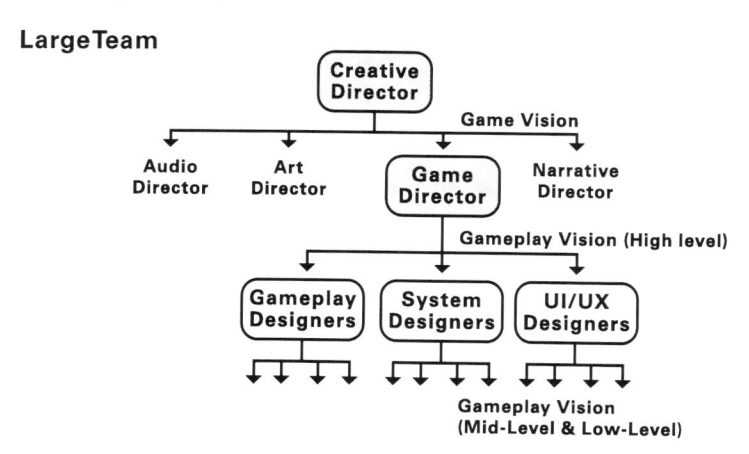

Large Team

```
                    Creative
                    Director
                       |
                       |      Game Vision
    ┌──────────┬───────┼──────────┐
    ↓          ↓       ↓          ↓
  Audio       Art     Game     Narrative
 Director  Director  Director   Director
                       |
                       | Gameplay Vision (High level)
           ┌───────────┼───────────┐
           ↓           ↓           ↓
        Gameplay     System      UI/UX
        Designers   Designers   Designers
          ↓↓↓↓       ↓↓↓↓        ↓↓↓↓
                 Gameplay Vision
                (Mid-Level & Low-Level)
```

Small Team

```
                    ┌──────────┐
                    │ Creative │
                    │ Director │
                    └────┬─────┘
         Game & Gameplay Vision (High-level)
     ↓      ↓        ↓        ↓
                ┌──────────┐
                │   Game   │
                │ Designer │
                └────┬─────┘
              ↓  ↓  ↓
       Gameplay Vision (Mid-Level & Low-level)
```

Equal Owners*

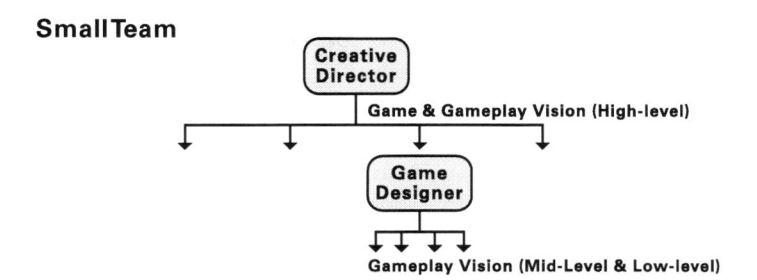

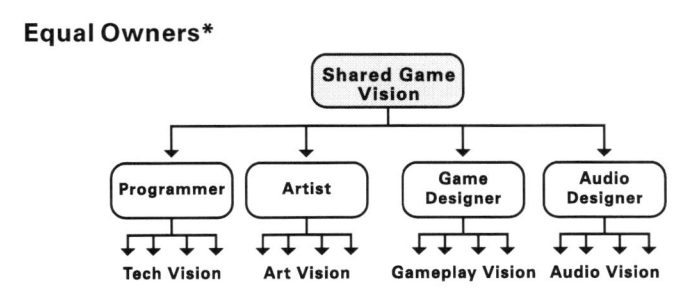

```
                    ┌──────────────┐
                    │ Shared Game  │
                    │    Vision    │
                    └──────┬───────┘
          ↓          ↓          ↓          ↓
    ┌──────────┐ ┌────────┐ ┌──────────┐ ┌──────────┐
    │Programmer│ │ Artist │ │   Game   │ │  Audio   │
    │          │ │        │ │ Designer │ │ Designer │
    └────┬─────┘ └───┬────┘ └────┬─────┘ └────┬─────┘
      ↓↓↓         ↓↓↓          ↓↓↓          ↓↓↓
   Tech Vision  Art Vision  Gameplay Vision  Audio Vision
```

*I've seen teams attempt equal ownership of the game vision but I've never seen it work.

Owning Vision

Vision is generally misconstrued as something only the higher-ups handle while everyone else focuses on developing the game. Vision isn't a magical divining rod used by directors to make big calls or changes during development. Vision is owned by the entire team and used by every member of the team to solve the day-to-day development problems.

> **Vision:** An understanding of how *all* the pieces will come together to create the experience.

Without an understanding of how the pieces will come together, how can we build an experience effectively? For example, why would you add Gadget B to your first-person

The Role of a Great Game Designer   59

shooter without an idea of what that gadget is bringing to the experience, how it connects to your other systems, and how it serves the goals of the overall game? Although building without a vision is possible, I would never recommend it. The teams I've seen go down that road usually end up redesigning their game multiple times and wasting a lot of effort. If you find yourself redesigning a feature, it's a good moment to stop and ask yourself if you understand the vision for the game, the vision for the gameplay experience, and how the feature connects to those two visions as well as to your other systems.

The term *all* in the vision definition should not be taken lightly. How can one person hope to comprehend how ALL the pieces of a game come together? Is the creative director expected to understand the bullet systems behind each weapon, the pathing priorities of each AI archetype, and the audio balance adjustments when switching from stealth to combat? If the entire team has only five people, then maybe. But if the team has over twenty developers, then there's very little chance. That's why the creative director focuses on building a high-level game vision for the overall game while allowing the team members to own the vision for their own disciplines. For the purposes of this book, we'll focus on the game vision set by the creative director and the gameplay vision owned by the game design team.

Game Vision

The game vision is the high-level vision for the overall game. In general, high-level visions consist of broader concepts that inspire a mental image of how the experience will come together. Those concepts are what all other linked visions and decisions will stem from. The goal is for every high-level vision to be clear, concise, and easily understood by the team.

The game vision is usually owned by the highest creative position on the team (creative director or executive producer, depending on the company). This vision should explain the game while also having hooks for each discipline to build off of (art, gameplay, audio, etc.). The following are elements of game vision used in the industry.

Vision Statement

At many studios, directors describe their game vision through one clear and concise sentence. These can be referred to as vision statements. Vision statements are meant to highlight the experience and key differentiator as quickly and cleanly as possible by using references everyone can easily understand. *Dead Space* (Electronic Arts, 2008) had one of the clearest game visions of any other team I've been a part of: *"Resident Evil 4* in Space." That simple statement allowed the team to easily hone in on the experience we were shooting for. If there was ever a question of which way to go on a feature, the response was usually "Which is more *Resident Evil 4* in Space?"

Vision statements are a powerful tool when used right. The trick to a solid vision statement is to keep it simple. A vision statement is not an elevator pitch. An elevator pitch is a sales pitch meant to explain a project's opportunity and key selling points. A vision statement is meant to inspire every discipline on the team. It's not meant to provide all the answers; instead, it serves as a guiding light.

Vision statements describe the desired experience by referencing experiences that already exist in the world. They can reference any medium. And the more the team understands the stated references, the more they'll understand what they're building toward. Some creatives may dislike calling their experience "Game X meets Movie Y" as they feel it instantly makes their vision derivative. But vision statements value clarity above all else. It's better that a team understand where it's going rather than the vision be utterly unique but mysterious. I've seen many teams block derivative discussions or terminology because they felt it hurt their uniqueness. But if you're afraid to talk about other products and terms, chances are you have insecurities and not uniqueness.

I highly recommend teams try out vision statements. Having a vision like "Genre X meets Book Y with Differentiator Z" instantly builds a strong list of references you want your team to become experts in. But make sure to define what you're hoping to take from each reference. And most importantly, get feedback from your team. Give them the vision statement and ask them to describe the experience back to you. Then describe what your intended experience is and discuss the differences. This process can lead to finding other references you didn't even know existed. In the end, you'll have a single statement that everyone can pull from when solving problems and developing their individual tasks.

Game Pillars

Pillars are individual, high-level concepts that highlight the major areas of focus the experience is based on. Most projects focus on three core pillars, but the pillars themselves aren't the important part. The most important piece is how these three pillars come together to make a cohesive, singular experience. I've seen projects that develop three pillars and stop there. But these concepts make very little sense until they are defined and woven together to describe the experience. Here's an example for *Splinter Cell: Blacklist*[2]:

> **Pillars:** Sam | Killing Ballet | Strategic Mission Interface (SMI)

[2] Richard Carrillo, *Building a Shared Vision with Directors & Teams,* Nordic Game, 2020

Sam: Sam Fisher is the main protagonist of the series. This game will center around him in every way. It's his story, his fight, and his decisions as he leads the new Fourth Echelon. He's no longer following any orders but his own.

Killing Ballet: We must focus on a fluid gameplay experience. Sam should be able to move through a room and engage every enemy without stopping. This fluidity should exist throughout the entire experience, from the start of a mission to the end.

SMI: The Strategic Mission Interface exists at the heart of Fourth Echelon and at the heart of the game. It's where all mission decisions are made and can be felt throughout the experience. It brings together all modes, progression, replayability, and companion apps.

Experience Description: In *Splinter Cell: Blacklist* we'll see a new Sam Fisher—a leader who runs his own team and makes the final call, an operative whose expertise makes him an unstoppable force as he moves fluidly through the battlefield, and a commander who uses the SMI to manage operations around the world. In *Splinter Cell: Blacklist,* you are not only Sam Fisher, you are Fourth Echelon.

Based on this example, we can see how each pillar taken on its own might cause confusion. Defining the pillars is required to ensure the team will comprehend the concepts. And more importantly, defining how these pillars combine to create the experience is needed to ensure a deeper understanding. With understanding, the team can move forward and take ownership of the questions and problems that will come up throughout development.

Creating solid game pillars can be a tough challenge. Pillars are about building alignment on the experience's foundation. Every feature, aesthetic, and decision during development should bring the experience closer to reaching the pillars. Here are some principles to follow when determining pillars:

- **Pillars should be useful to every discipline.** A pillar should never be so specific that it is only useful to a select few areas of development (art, audio, gameplay, etc.). Pillars are meant to align the entire team, and going too specific can lead to certain areas having no guiding light to follow. For example, 60 frames per second (fps) is not a good pillar. It may be a solid goal you want to accomplish, but 60 fps is very specific to a few disciplines and could be achieved by just one (engine programming). Each pillar should help define the experience and inspire the *entire* team.

    Although a pillar should never serve only one discipline, it is okay for pillars to lean toward an individual discipline. The Killing Ballet pillar leans heavily toward gameplay, but the push for fluidity in the experience can be used by every discipline on the team.

- **Don't go too broad or generic.** Pillars are meant to bring alignment on a single experience. The pillars "grounded," "social," and "online" do very little to inspire a single experience. Pillars are about inspiration and not just stating important concepts. If you've gone too broad, try defining what that pillar means to you. This can help you develop a stronger pillar. For example, if "social" mostly revolves around building an in-game community, then maybe "building an in-game community" is a stronger pillar. Of course, you'll still need to further define what "in-game community" means for the experience.

- **Think *mood, world,* and *experience*.** I've found that focusing one pillar on each of these three concepts can generate a well-rounded game vision. The mood pillar should define what you want the player to feel. The world pillar focuses on setting and what makes it stand out. The experience pillar should focus on action or fantasy—who the player is and what they're doing.

These principles have helped me to better define the experiences I've worked on, but they aren't the only path to successful pillars. What's important is to iterate with the team. The entire point of the game vision is to ensure the team understands and believes in the direction they're heading.

Game Goals

Every game usually has a set of high-level goals the higher-ups want to achieve with the experience. These are all part of the game vision, and it's important for the team to fully understand and believe in them. Here's an example for *Splinter Cell: Blacklist:*

> **Appeal to the Shooter Market:** Historically, the *Splinter Cell* brand has focused on the hardcore stealth market. With *Splinter Cell: Conviction,* the team opened up the experience to a wider audience by focusing on lethal stealth. We want *SC: Blacklist* to take it further and open the experience to all third-person shooter fans while not alienating the stealth or lethal stealth markets.

Game goals are directed more toward tackling individual challenges, like hitting a specific market, integrating a unique technology, or maintaining 60 fps throughout development. They are an important aspect of the vision and are a bit easier to change during development than are pillars or the vision statement.

Bringing the Game Vision Together

Vision statements, pillars, and game goals are a few of the game vision elements I've worked with in my career. Additional elements most likely exist. Regardless, they all have the same purpose: to inspire the team and align them on the experience they're creating. The goal isn't to sound cool or wow the cameras. It's simply to ensure understanding and belief. Without understanding, everyone is walking in different directions. Without belief, developers lose passion and the end product suffers. Although the game vision is owned by the top creative seat, they should still utilize their entire conception team (usually under twenty devs) for brainstorming and feedback.

A strong high-level vision that the team believes in is invaluable. It leads to a team all working together toward the same goal without a lot of oversight needed. That, in turn, creates the feeling of ownership. I've always found that if a team has many micromanaging directors, it's usually because the vision isn't strong enough. The more a team doesn't understand where they are going, the more likely they are to build something that doesn't fit. The more that happens, the less directors will trust them. This spirals into horrible micromanaging conditions initially sparked by poor high-level direction.

To all directors, if you find a team member developing something that doesn't jive with the vision, then you must ask yourselves, "Where is the vision failing? How is it being misinterpreted? How can I make it more clear?"

Gameplay Vision

The gameplay vision is an understanding of how all the pieces come together to create the gameplay experience. This vision is owned by the entire game design team, not just the designers at the top. With a strong gameplay vision, every developer who touches gameplay will be able to make correct day-to-day decisions, without a lot of oversight. As with all discipline-focused visions, the gameplay vision is an offshoot of the game vision and can be broken into three sections: high-level, mid-level, and low-level.

High-Level Gameplay Vision

The high-level gameplay vision is owned by the highest member of the game design hierarchy, usually a game director or lead game designer. The goal is to translate the overall game vision from the creative director into what it means for the gameplay experience. I've seen teams on which each director tries to come up with a unique set of pillars. This tends to create more silos and less of a cohesive experience. It's important to build all visions off of the core game vision. Defining how that vision translates into your discipline will ensure everything stays aligned.

The intention is to build a clear and concise high-level vision that the entire team can understand while also leaving it open enough to allow for the game design team to own the mid-level and low-level visions. It should inspire, not prescribe. We'll now consider an example based on the *Splinter Cell: Blacklist* game vision we discussed earlier.

Splinter Cell: Blacklist

Pillar Translation. The first step in creating a high-level vision for a discipline is to translate the game vision for that discipline. Starting with the pillars, the director must ask, "What does this pillar mean for my discipline?"

> **Game Vision Pillars:** Sam | Killing Ballet | Strategic Mission Interface (SMI)
>
> **Sam → Ultimate Spy:** Sam Fisher is the ultimate spy, and what we're delivering is the ultimate spy fantasy. This means high-tech gadgets, cutting edge weaponry, and a strong focus on infiltration. The player should feel like their arsenal allows them to remain in control no matter the situation.
>
> **Killing Ballet → Fluid Nav & Combat:** Moving through enemies should feel like a dance, with the player's momentum never slowing. The player should feel unleashed and not restricted by animations or clunky systems. By planning their actions and choosing their moment, the player can string together kills and clear a room without being stopped. We'll give them the tools, but it will take their tactics and skill to pull it off.
>
> **SMI → Progression & Economy:** Although they may seem simple, progression and economy systems have never been a part of the *Splinter Cell* franchise before. For us, these systems will focus on increasing player autonomy and adding an extra layer of strategy before and during each mission. The player should be able to play the way they want and progress the way they want, ensuring they are building their Fourth Echelon.
>
> **Gameplay Experience:** You are the ultimate spy. Your training in weapons, infiltration, and espionage allows

you to operate flawlessly behind enemy lines. Take your time, plan your advance, and clear each room with ease. You call the shots and reap the rewards as you advance your command center to access cutting-edge tools to help you overcome the next hurdle.

These become the major focal points for that discipline. Each designer should develop towards this experience while also keeping the overall game vision in mind.

Goal Translation. The second step is translating the game goals in terms of what they mean for the gameplay experience. Each director will translate these goals into something for their own field. Here's an example based on the Broader Market Appeal goal we discussed earlier:

> **Broader Market Appeal → Assault Playstyle:** The *Splinter Cell* brand is known for its ghost and panther playstyles. With ghost, players can stealth a mission so flawlessly there is no sign they were ever there. With panther, players can clear rooms of enemies by attacking from the shadows and vanishing before others notice. In *Splinter Cell: Blacklist,* we will continue to support these playstyles while also adding a third style: assault. Assault players will be able to go loud and stay loud, using their superior firepower and precision skills to take out enemies quickly and efficiently. All three playstyles will challenge different player skills and be fully supported in our loadout and progression systems. With these three playstyles, players will truly be able to play the full experience their way.

Gameplay Loops. The high-level gameplay vision should also define the game loop and gameplay loops. Although the owner of this vision makes the final call, it's important to collect input from every game designer and ensure their buy-in. Here are some *Blacklist* examples of the game loop and a couple levels of gameplay loops:

> **Game Loop:** Command > Engage > Advance
>
> **Command:** Take command of Fourth Echelon, choose your mission, and build your loadout.
>
> **Engage:** Complete the mission the way you want. You're in control from start to finish.
>
> **Advance:** Success brings its own rewards. Upgrade your command center to better outfit yourself for the next operation.
>
> **Game Loop Experience:** The player's objective is to take command of Fourth Echelon, bring down the main antagonist, and save the world. Their challenge lies in completing each mission. As missions become more challenging, players will need to upgrade their command center and their gear. The reward is game completion and the conclusion of the narrative.
>
> **Engage Gameplay Loop:** Plan > Execute > Vanish
>
> **Plan:** Take your time and plan out each encounter. Will you utilize the environment, distract your opponents, or just take them out?
>
> **Execute:** Enact your plan with skill and precision.
>
> **Vanish:** Disappear and ready yourself for your next encounter.

Ghost Experience: The ghost player's objective is to complete the mission or encounter with nobody knowing they were there. The challenge is getting through each enemy encounter without being spotted by or engaging with a single enemy. The reward is the economy gain for each successful encounter and advancing to the next encounter/mission.

Panther Experience: The panther player's objective is to complete the mission or encounter by taking down all enemy threats without being spotted. The challenge is engaging with each enemy before being spotted. The reward is the economy gain for each successful encounter and advancing to the next encounter/mission.

Assault Experience: The assault player's objective is to complete the mission or encounter through tactical military combat. The challenge is getting through each enemy encounter unscathed and working their way from objective to objective with precision as enemy reinforcements enter the field. The reward is the economy gain for each successful encounter and advancing to the next encounter/mission.

Plan Gameplay Loop: Spot > Track > Strategize

Spot: Find enemies and opportunities while hidden in the shadows. Use vision modes to take in the full picture of the challenges ahead.

Track: Track targets, notice their patterns, and discover windows.

Strategize: With information as the reward, make a plan of attack or evasion. Wait for the right moment. Everything will need to be timed out perfectly.

Plan Experience: The player's objective is to fully understand the encounter and build a successful plan of attack before engaging. The challenge lies with spotting all enemies or traps and being able to identify a practical pattern while taking into account their current gear and capabilities. The reward is understanding the challenge ahead and having a promising plan to enter the next beat of Execute.

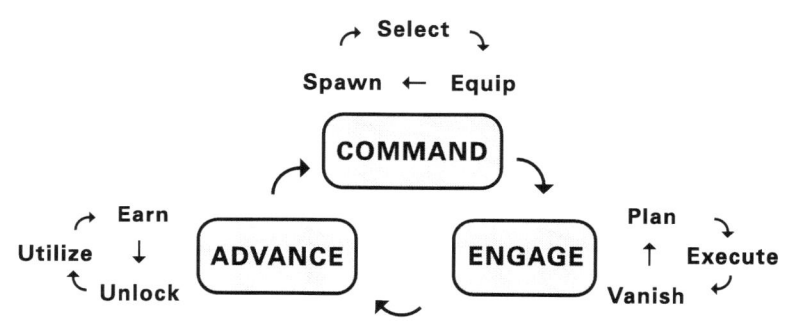

```
              ↗ Select ↘
        Spawn ← Equip
              ┌─────────┐
            ↗ │ COMMAND │ ↘
              └─────────┘
    ↗ Earn                              Plan ↘
Utilize ↓  ┌─────────┐    ┌────────┐  ↑      Execute
    ↖ Unlock │ ADVANCE │    │ ENGAGE │         ↙
           └─────────┘    └────────┘  Vanish
                      ↖         ↙
```

With the game vision translated and the gameplay loops designed, the high-level gameplay vision must still be validated by all directors and designers and communicated to the full team in a clear and concise way. After that, the design team must champion and police that vision to ensure all pieces are coming together into a cohesive and compelling experience. This vision will be the guiding light for designers who own the mid-level gameplay vision.

Mid-Level Gameplay Vision

The mid-level gameplay vision offers a stronger understanding of how each specialty within the gameplay experience comes together and connects to the high-level gameplay vision (i.e., AI, combat, progression). Mid-level vision is generally owned by a senior or expert developer within that specialty. Building off of what we already discussed, here's an example for AI in *Splinter Cell: Blacklist*.

Splinter Cell: Blacklist

AI Goals.

> **Ultimate Spy for AI:** The AI enemies are the counterpoints to the ultimate spy. Each individual archetype must offer a compelling and unique challenge against one or more tools in Sam's arsenal. Each archetype must also have at least one weakness to be exploited by each playstyle (ghost, panther, assault).
>
> **Fluid Nav & Combat for AI:** When the player plans out their tactical approach to an encounter, AI position, pathing, and archetype should all be major factors that will impact a player's plan. Clearing a room fluidly should be a puzzle with the AI being the major pieces.
>
> **Progression & Economy for AI:** AI archetypes should offer a progression from mission to mission that provides a deeper challenge and helps drive the player's decisions in their own progression.
>
> **Plan > Execute > Vanish for AI:** Each beat of the core gameplay loop should be challenged by our AI archetypes.

Every AI Designer must keep these goals in mind as they design out the AI archetypes and features. They must also understand and maintain the high-level gameplay vision goals as well as the game vision goals and pillars.

Low-Level Gameplay Vision

The low-level gameplay vision is a detailed understanding of what each individual feature will bring to the experience, including its goals and how it fits in the gameplay experience and loops. Following is an example of low-level vision for a new AI archetype in *Splinter Cell: Blacklist*.

Splinter Cell: Blacklist

New Enemy Archetype. Requests came for a new enemy archetype due to a problem witnessed in the experience. We didn't have an enemy that challenged the plan beat of the core gameplay loop. And with no challenge, that phase of the experience was becoming too predictable and unengaging. One way to develop the low-level gameplay vision is to create goals based on the core gameplay loop.

> **Core Gameplay Loop: Plan > Execute > Vanish**
>
> **Plan Goal:** The new archetype should disrupt the player's ability to spot and track enemies, causing the player to deal with this archetype or risk entering the situation without a plan.
>
> **Execute Goal:** The new archetype should focus on the plan and vanish phases and therefore offer a lower 1:1 challenge in the execute phase.
>
> **Vanish Goal:** The new archetype should make it more difficult for Sam to remain hidden, therefore creating more tension during the plan phase.

By focusing the challenge during the plan and vanish stages and reducing the challenge during the execute stage, we allow more tactics to present themselves when players face many archetypes at once. Based on the player's playstyle, they will each have different priorities even though they face the same enemy setup. All of this is aligned with the first two AI goals discussed in the mid-level gameplay vision.

Enemy Design: Tech Archetype. These goals sparked discussions and the design that led to the creation of a new enemy archetype. The tech archetype would disrupt Sam's vision modes and spawn radio-controlled (RC) drones that are on a constant hunt for the player. This archetype validated all goals and was a successful addition to the experience in a development cycle in which hundreds of successful additions come together every month.

Bringing the Gameplay Vision Together

The gameplay vision has a lot of moving parts, and it takes the entire design team to pull it together and keep it together. Without a solid vision you may notice a lot of features diverging and having trouble fusing into a cohesive experience. You'll see developers making decisions that lead to a different experience and don't belong. And you'll have a lot of team members asking you every day, "What is the game?" Hundreds of decisions are made daily all across the team. The only way to ensure every decision is driving toward the same experience is to have a strong enough vision that the team believes in.

The role of the game designer is to own the gameplay vision and ensure all the designs are coming together toward the same gameplay experience. The vision should rarely change. Instead, it's the designs that take the brunt of heavy iteration and so getting the team to believe in the vision is more important than the designs themselves. And collaborating with the team on the designs is more important than any individual thoughts and ideas. Doing all of this right will foster a dev team whose passion will drive the project to success. Doing it wrong can create a spiraling world of fires, micromanagement, wasted effort, complete redesign, and a lot of developer turnover.

We are all here because of our passion for making great games. That passion must be encouraged or it will fade. Game designers are at the core of inspiring that passion in the team.

PART TWO

● ●

PROCESS

CHAPTER 4

THE GAME DESIGN PROCESS

In Part One of this book we defined *game* and *game design* and introduced the game designer as the owner of the gameplay vision. In Part Two we will discuss the process of taking features from vision to finalized design. Leading this process is a big part of the game designer's job. It's how they drive the gameplay experience and where most of their day to day is spent.

Beginning with the game design definition set in Chapter 2, our purpose is to facilitate play through fantasy and mechanics while utilizing rules and systems to create challenge and opposition to the player's goal. That's the basics of what we want to achieve, but how do we go about achieving it?

Most people believe the first step of the design process is coming up with ideas. This is not the case. Many people fantasize about becoming game designers because they feel they have great ideas for games. But the truth is that everyone has great ideas and game design is not about coming up with them.

The Problem with Ideas

Many developers in the video game industry consider ideas cheap or worthless. These people are generally reflecting the view that implementation is king (and it is) and that ideation is easy. The process of implementing an idea, in any field, will always raise tons of questions and even more problems that need to be solved. So coming up with ideas really means creating more questions and more problems. This is why nobody wants an "idea person" on their team.

From a game design perspective, there is another angle to consider. An idea is not part of a game until it is formed into a rule, mechanic, or system. Any game idea you've ever had is rife with problems as you try to insert it into the experience. Anyone clinging to the hope that they have the *perfect idea* is missing a major point. There is no such thing as a perfect idea. In my experience, countless ideas can work to fill the void in the current design. Success comes down to the *implementation* of the idea and how it's weaved into the rest of the experience through development and iteration.

Although ideas can be considered cheap or worthless, there is one thing worse—something that can actually hurt the game. This is the dreaded "cool" idea, or an idea that sounds exciting but doesn't fit in the current systems or gameplay loops of the experience. These ideas can take hold of dev teams that are tired of looking at the same game for two plus years. They derail the development and set the team on snipe hunts. Some of the biggest headaches I've had to deal with have come from joining teams that have hundreds of cool ideas and no game. Imagine an experience filled with individual prototypes but no purpose. Each idea was a cool toy that led to its own distinct play but not to a cohesive experience. Understanding your gameplay loops is really your first line of defense against too many random cool ideas plaguing your experience and your development.

In short, ideas can range from cheap to devastating. Everyone has ideas and building a list of ideas is easy, but finding the right idea for the right situation is hard. Notice that I said "finding the right idea" and not "thinking up one." Game design is not about ideation. Ideas are everywhere: in every mind, every game, and every experience. Everyone has ideas. Game design is about being open to all ideas from every source and honing in on the ones needed to solve the current problem at hand. Game design is about problem solving.

The Problem-Solving Process

One of the goals when completing any type of task is to develop a process that a person can reuse effectively. This ensures that our results and successes can be repeated. When thinking of game design as solving problems, the entire process gains more focus. Every step toward reaching the vision is a problem that needs to be solved. Focusing on problem solving ensures all the designs are building toward that one solid experience. It also allows us to use the greatest problem-solving process available: the scientific method. Don't worry: This won't feel like science class in the end. Most designers are already using this method without realizing it. But fully identifying it allows us to perfect our process. The scientific method is structured as follows:

1. Observe/question
2. Build a hypothesis
3. Test the hypothesis
4. Analyze data
5. Draw conclusion

Rethinking this process specifically for game design, we get the following:

1. Observe/question
   - Identify the problem
   - Build goals
2. Build a hypothesis
   - Maximize ideas
   - Design the solution
3. Test the hypothesis
   - Prototype the solution
   - Playtest the solution
4. Analyze data
   - Analyze playtest results
5. Draw conclusion
   - Finalize or iterate

Here is the final process influenced by the scientific method:

1. Identify the problem
2. Build goals
3. Maximize ideas
4. Design the solution
5. Prototype the solution
6. Playtest the solution
7. Analyze playtest results
8. Finalize or iterate

This may seem like a lot of steps, but each one is needed and in this order. The more you utilize this process, the faster it will all become. Most designers will find they already do this but have never spelled it out in this way. For the rest of Part Two, we will step through each beat in this process and solve an example design problem along the way.

CHAPTER 5

IDENTIFY THE PROBLEM

Everything in game design can be thought of as a problem you're trying to solve. Of course, before you can solve any problem, you need to correctly identify it. In game design, we identify problems through research and observation. Let's look at the most common types of problems you'll face.

New Game Problem

At the start of a project you should have a vision for the experience you want to create. This vision is your experiential goal and not a list of features. The problem is that your vision is not a game. Solving this problem means taking that first step into development. You don't have a playable game until you develop its most basic mechanics. This is always the start of the development process and the first problem you need to solve.

What are the basic player verbs that will start you down the path of building your core gameplay loop? If you want to develop a first-person shooter, then the first problem you may want to tackle could be *movement* or *shooting.* Getting the core verbs working is the first step to reaching your vision. Nowadays, most game engines have many of the basic verbs already available. But if the way they work is counter to your vision, then that may be the first problem you need to solve.

Developing games is about creating experiences. Don't focus on documentation for too long. Focusing on the experience will get you much further. What is the first mechanic that's keeping you from to attaining your vision? What problem are you trying to solve?

New Feature Problem

New feature requests pop up often when you're developing a game. Maybe this is your first feature in the experience, maybe you already have a list of features you know you want in the game, or maybe a developer on the team has come up with something new that everyone agrees the game needs. No matter how the feature request came about, the first step is the same. You must ask yourself, "What problem is this feature trying to solve?" It may seem simple, but once you dive into this question, you'll realize that the answer helps keep the feature focused and leads to better designs.

For example, a director may suggest that your game needs a progression system. But what problem is this trying to solve? Or, thought another way, what would happen if you didn't add this feature?

- Does the game have so many player mechanics that the player is overwhelmed and, therefore, it's beneficial to unlock the mechanics over time instead of all at once?

- Does the experience have different player archetypes/classes that need to be differentiated through ability unlocks?
- Does the game need a simple retention system to ensure the player always has a reason to return?
- Is it a free-to-play experience that needs deep hooks to always keep the player dreaming about the next step and whether or not to spend money?

This questioning approach defines the need before attempting the design. It also ensures the feature has an inherent motivation for the player to actually use it. If you simply focus on the request, such as "We're making a role-playing game (RPG) so we need experience point (XP) gains and levels," features will end up feeling tacked on and shallow. There are quite a few successful RPGs that don't have XP or levels, so why does this game need them? What problem are you trying to solve?

Broken Gameplay Problem

The most common problem game designers face is that of something in the game just not working out. Such problems will be revealed through either qualitative or quantitative analysis.

- Qualitative issues are first identified by the feeling that something is wrong. For example, players may find a specific puzzle frustrating.
- Quantitative issues occur when the data don't match the expected results. For example, players aren't using grenades even though they were expected to use at least one per mission.

These types of problems can cause you to jump quickly to a conclusion, but research, observation, and critical thinking are required to identify the actual root causes. This is why play testers can help you identify that a problem exists, but they might be way off with their proposed solutions. Even so, what players feel and experience is still very important. It's up to game designers and user researchers to take their observations further through the following steps:

1. Observe Negative Results

As mentioned earlier, negative results are revealed through either qualitative or quantitative analysis.

- Qualitative: A player had a negative experience. You'll first want to understand how many players feel the same and if the negative experiences are negatively affecting the overall fun or appreciation of the game.

- Quantitative: Players aren't experiencing the game the way you expected them to. Is this hurting the overall fun or appreciation? Is appreciation expected to increase if we push them toward the expected experience?

It's on the designer, user researcher, and directors to determine if a negative result needs to be acted on. Decisions are usually based on how many players had the issue and if appreciation of the experience is low enough to require action.

2. Identify the Problem

What is the negative player experience that's occurring? The problem should always be identified in the simplest terms, from the player's perspective. For example, the problem might be that players aren't using grenades when developers expected them to.

Be careful not to jump ahead too quickly. Too often I've seen developers identify a cause or a solution instead of the problem. The problem is that players aren't using grenades. It isn't that there aren't enough enemy setups that push grenade use. This is a possible *cause* of the problem. Neither is it that we need better indicators to show grenades available. This is a possible *solution* to a problem. These two examples skip important steps in the discussion. By skipping steps in the problem-solving process, you may find yourself endlessly iterating without solving the problem.

3. Identify the Cause

What's the root cause of the problem—and remember that there may be multiple causes? This is where you dive deep into mechanics and systems to lay out what you believe is actually creating the issue. Your conclusion in this step is your first hypothesis, and it will help you build your testable solution. But as with any hypothesis, it may be incorrect.

> **Hypothesis**: I believe players aren't using grenades because they never learned how to use them or they don't know that they even exist.

Find as much data as you can to back up your hypothesis. In our example about the grenades, let's say you have noticed that players looked confused when asked how they felt about the grenades. Or maybe quantitative data showed that players who used grenades once ended up using them frequently, but most players never used them even once.

4. Find a Solution

Only after you have hypothesized the cause can you move on through the design process to search for a solution.

Focusing on problem solving is the easiest way to get a team to believe in a design. To ensure belief, you'll need to convince them the problem exists, that it needs to be solved, and that your design is the optimal solution. Always work in that order and don't move on to the next beat until the team is convinced. Taking this care will go much further with the team than the "Trust me, I'm the designer" approach.

By focusing on game design in terms of solving problems, you also ensure that you're adding a net gain to the experience, getting closer to the vision and to a finished product. In contrast, focusing on ideation as your driving factor will open countless subjective topics that will continue to send you down new and unknown paths. Although that may sound exciting on small teams, it is detrimental to larger ones.

In Chapter 2 we discussed the game *Rock, Paper, Scissors, Lizard, Spock* and identified a problem within that experience. As we go through the game design process in Part Two, we'll also use this process on the RPSLS problem to find a solution:

Rock, Paper, Scissors, Lizard, Spock
Identify the Problem

Rock, Paper, Scissors, Lizard, Spock (RPSLS) is a five-option version of Rock, Paper, Scissors. It's perfectly balanced with each option having two win conditions and two loss conditions. The inputs (hand gestures) for each option are easy to understand and different enough from each other to quickly distinguish them. The problem can be witnessed after a few play sessions:

> **Qualitative Issue:** RPSLS is difficult to play. Because there are so many options, it's hard to remember what beats what.

As we discussed earlier (and can be found through research), games like *Pokémon* have many more options but are somehow easier to manage. David C. Lovelace also created a 101-option RPS that is impossible to manage in a standard RPS setting. At this point we need to make more observations before we can correctly identify the problem in RPSLS. We can start by asking which interactions are difficult to remember.

> **Problem:** It's difficult to remember what options Spock wins against and loses against.

The output for Lizard is straightforward. It gets crushed by Rock, gets decapitated by Scissors (I prefer *skewered*), and eats through Paper. So why can't Spock eat through paper? Because when it comes to Spock, Paper suddenly becomes a logical argument that disproves Spock. Spock also uses his phaser to vaporize Rock but seems to not have his phaser when interacting with any of the other options (especially Lizard). Most of the interactions between Spock and the other options are references to the *Star Trek* series. But the references aren't the issue. The hypothesized cause of the problem is as follows:

> **Hypothesis:** The Spock option creates fantasy incongruity. The fantasy with how Spock interacts with the other options is unique for each option and can even alter the original fantasy for that option. This makes it hard to keep track of the interactions.

Changing the fantasy of an option within the same system obfuscates its purpose. If Paper can now mean *logical argument*, why can't Rock mean *planet?* Why does Spock vaporize Rock but can't vaporize Lizard? When did the Lizard become poisonous? The simplicity of the original *Rock, Paper, Scissors* was that each option was exactly what it was named.

Now that we've identified the problem and hypothesized the cause we can move onto the next step of the process.

The Role of a Great Game Designer

CHAPTER 6

BUILD GOALS

Design goals are one of the most important steps of the design process, and it's sadly the step I've seen game designers miss most often. Every design you create should begin with goals it's trying to achieve. There are three major reasons for this:

- **Alignment**: Goals align everyone on the team with the purpose of the design. Whether they're for a brainstorm meeting or a design pitch, goals ensure everyone is on the same page about what they're working to achieve. Also, when goals are in focus, the discussion around a design's success won't end up layered in subjectivity; instead it will revolve around how well the design achieves the goals.

- **Reinforcement**: Goals ensure the design doesn't deviate from its original purpose in the future. Every day different team members will question designs that have already been implemented. This is a sign of a healthy team environment. The best response to these questions is, "This design accomplishes the following goals. Do we still believe in these goals? Is it still accomplishing these goals?" This response will either reinforce the design or start a constructive conversation on which goals the design is failing to achieve or why a change in goals is needed.

- **Validation:** Goals should always be written in a way that can be validated through playtests. When they're not, we can't determine if we've achieved our goals. For example, "retention" is not a good goal for a feature, but "Increase Day 7 retention by 100 percent" is a huge goal for a feature and something verifiable (at least post-launch).

Now that we understand the intentions, let's discuss what design goals are and how to create them. In the past, I've seen many designers confuse high-level goals and low-level requirements. "Players should use an AK-47 during this encounter" is a low-level requirement and not a goal. On the other hand, "this feature should push players to use automatic weapons" is a great goal.

Goals are broad, high-level statements. They should feel like opportunities and not restrictions. Goals aren't the solution; they are additional problems you're trying to solve. They should be easy to understand and even easier to agree on. And most importantly, your goals should inspire. They should inspire ideas and inspire the team to believe in the feature. Each design should have around three to five high-level goals. The highest priority goal should be obvious:

> **Goal #1:** Solving the cause of your primary problem and, therefore, the problem itself.

If the feature doesn't end up solving the cause of your problem, then it failed. It's also possible it resolved the cause but not the problem, meaning you either misidentified the cause or the problem is more complex and has multiple causes. Complex problems may need multiple solutions working together.

Here are some other types of goals:

- Maintaining the vision for the overall game
- Engaging certain markets, player types, or player behaviors
- Solving other lesser problems at the same time
- Ensuring that new, specific problems aren't created
- Upholding a fantasy or pushing a specific feel
- Reaching a specified benchmark metric to determine success

When building a new feature, your first set of goals will generally come from the director level (creative director, game director, etc.). As a game designer, you need to own and understand all the goals for your features. But at times, directors may push solutions instead of goals or visions. If this is the case, then you need to simply respond with "What problem are you trying to solve?" Force the discussion into addressing the high-level goals you are trying to achieve and **make sure you're not getting sidetracked by solutions**.

After receiving the initial set of director goals, it's on the game designer to **finalize the list of goals and ensure team buy-in**.

When finalizing your goals, another important aspect is to **ensure no two goals conflict with each other.** Conflicting goals can cause headaches and keep you from finding a workable solution. They can also be hard to spot until you're deep in development and frustrated with your feature. The easiest way to overcome the problem of conflicting goals is to list your goals in priority order. As long as the team understands the priorities, they will find it easier to make concessions and even remove some conflicting goals later on.

Most disagreements around the success of a feature tend to be caused by teammates and directors having different priorities. I've seen discussions go in circles for hours due to this issue. It's on designers to **ensure a prioritized list of goals**. Never accept "We want it all" as a response to prioritization.

Maintaining strong goals and priorities is one of the most important aspects of game design. It is always the first thing I inspect when engaging with teams that are having design issues. I will generally care less about the design itself and more about how they designed it because millions of designs could work, and choosing among them is mostly subjective. But did team members set themselves up for success throughout the design process? Did they identify the problem, identify its cause, and develop appropriate design goals? Does the team believe that the problem exists and that it needs to be solved? Do the design goals inspire the team? Are their goals prioritized? The importance of this step cannot be overstated.

Rock, Paper, Scissors, Lizard, Spock
Build Goals

The original goal that led to the creation of five-option RPSLS was to reduce the number of tie games in RPS due to both players throwing the same option. This is still a valid goal for the overall experience, but the design created the following problem we identified:

> It's difficult to remember what options Spock wins against and loses against.

We next identified a hypothetical cause:

> The Spock option creates fantasy incongruity. The fantasy with how Spock interacts with the other options is unique for each option and can even alter the original fantasy for that option. This makes it hard to keep track of the interactions.

Now we must develop the design goals for our solution to the hypothesized cause.

> **Goal 1:** Create an easily memorizable five-option system by never altering fantasy between options and their interactions.
>
> **Goal 2:** Maintain the perfect balance of RPS, with each option having an equivalent number of win states and loss states.
>
> **Goal 3:** Ensure each hand gesture is easy to understand, is easily identifiable, and is distinguishable from the other gestures.

These goals will keep us on track and will help to ensure we aren't overcomplicating RPS and losing out on what made it so successful in the first place.

CHAPTER 7

MAXIMIZE IDEAS

In game design, every problem has a solution. In fact, every problem has millions of possible solutions. You'd assume that finding one of these million solutions would be easy except that there are billions of designs that won't work. These odds aren't good. And yet I've seen a lot of designers take their first idea, flesh it out, and push it through the process. The first step to combating these odds is to maximize the number of ideas before choosing one.

I know what you're thinking. I said that game design is not about ideation. And it isn't. This part isn't about you coming up with a ton of ideas. It's about you searching through as many ideas as possible and determining which one best solves the problem while fitting your systems and goals. These ideas can be found by analyzing other games & mediums (movies, books, activities, etc.), through discussions, and through brainstorms.

I know. You're excited about building an experience. But you have to fight the urge to take your first idea and iterate in engine. This is a trap. It's more likely that first idea exists in the billions of solutions that won't work. But through implementation you'll become married to it and hit the sunk cost fallacy: You've already put time into it, so now it feels like a waste of your investment to just let it go. Your colleagues will grow concerned as you continue to hammer a square peg into a round hole. They'll pitch you alternate solutions but because you're so invested you'll become defensive. "They just don't get it," you'll say. "But they'll see. They'll all see. Mwhahahaha!" When did you become the villain? The moment you picked your first idea, didn't get input from the team, and ignored all feedback.

Game dev is a team effort. And the best way to ensure your success is to maximize your ideas and include the team every step of the way. You'll always get a better result when more minds are working together toward a solution. So let's start searching for ideas.

Analyzing Other Games & Mediums

The trick in searching other sources for ideas is not to stop once you come across an idea you like. This is when the analysis actually begins. Now you must do a deep dive into how that idea is designed and connected to all its other systems. The analysis ends once you have the answers to the following questions:

- **Design Analysis**
  - How are they using this idea?
  - What mechanics and systems exist due to this idea or are altered by it?

- **Problem Analysis**
  - What problem was this idea solving?
  - If this idea was removed, what systems would fail? What problems would arise?

- **Goal Analysis**
    - What goals did the team have that led to this idea?
    - Where were games in this genre before this idea came about?
    - What did this idea change?

The purpose of these questions is to end with a list of goals that may have led to the creation of the reference's systems. All of this will help you strengthen your own goals. If you can, search out other sources with similar ideas and do the same with those. Then you'll be able to see how those two experiences and goals branched out from each other based on different needs.

Once you have the goals from these other sources, you can compare them to your own. The differences in goals will reveal how different your end product will be. One of their differentiating goals may have led them to create a few systems that you will not need. But if you remove those systems, does the whole design fall apart? On the other hand, could your unique goals be integrated into their design? Asking these questions can reveal major design holes that may have gone unnoticed until much later in development. So the next time someone says their design will simply "copy" a feature from another game, make sure they understand the complexities of what they are saying.

Discussions

Before starting any idea-generating conversation with another person, you'll always want to make sure you're on the same page regarding the problem you're trying to solve. Do they agree that there is a problem and that it needs to be solved? Do they agree on the cause of the problem? Do they agree with the design goals you've outlined? Don't worry about getting bogged down in these questions before the ideas start flowing. If you don't agree on the fundamentals, then the ideas will be less relevant. And above all else, remember that the objective isn't to get them to agree with your interpretations of those points. If they don't, then that's where the conversation must linger until you both come to a consensus. This impasse may lead to you altering your problem, cause, or goals. As designers, we must always be open to new insights on the problem at hand.

Once you're on the same page with the problem, cause, and goals, it's time to ask your collaborator for their thoughts on possible solutions. Any idea they pitch may be wrapped up in other goals they're bringing to the table. Focus on their goals for hidden gems to incorporate in your current list. Try to listen and only bring up your ideas when the conversation dies down. Other than that, try to keep their ideas alive by adding to them with thoughts of your own.

Remember, the purpose of these conversations is to source ideas, not only to talk about yours.

Brainstorms

Brainstorms can be a great source of ideas to solve your problem. The goal of a brainstorm is to capture as many ideas as possible. Although it's good to allow your mind to think freely during a brainstorm, you must also make sure it stays on task. Successful brainstorms have constraints. Open brainstorms without constraints lead to ideas that are rarely useful and meetings that end up feeling like a waste of time. Constraints allow people to be purposefully creative and, as the designer, you are in charge of bringing these constraints. The good news is we already have them outlined. They are our goals.

Although a person can successfully brainstorm alone, I always recommend involving more minds in the process. A brainstorm is a great moment to involve the team. More specifically, you should involve directors, game designers, the devs who will implement the final design, and a wildcard or two. I've been a part of successful brainstorms with as few as three people and as many as fifteen. The numbers don't matter as long as you manage time effectively and ensure everyone gets a chance to share their ideas.

Here's a successful format that has worked for me in the past:

1. **Present Topic:** Start by presenting the problem at hand, the cause, and your goals. It's always good to give a couple of example ideas to make sure everyone understands how it can all come together. Use imagery as much as possible to inspire and get the ideas flowing. Make sure this presentation ends with a one-slide recap that stays up during the brainstorm for quick reference.

2. **Brainstorm:** Hold a 10-minute quiet brainstorm during which each person writes their ideas on sticky notes.

3. **Share Ideas:** Each person goes to the front of the room one at a time, pitches their ideas, and sticks them on a board. It's good to keep similar ideas next to each other. This ends once all ideas are revealed and posted.

4. **Vote:** Each person gets three votes to vote for their favorite ideas. Votes are cast by people marking the sticky notes with a dot or star. When finished, add up the votes to determine the ideas most liked by the team.

5. **Conclude:** Game design should never be determined by committee nor should it happen in a vacuum. The purpose up to this point was to acquire a list of ideas that could lead to a solution. Voting helps the team express themselves

and helps to showcase which ideas are more compelling. Scope should also be considered: Make sure to consult the appropriate engineers and artists to remove or rethink any ideas that are too far out of scope.

At the end of this process, you should have a few workable ideas that could help solve your problem and may fit your goals. It isn't time to choose one just yet. After all, these are just ideas, not designs.

Rock, Paper, Scissors, Lizard, Spock
Maximize Ideas

For RPSLS we determined our problem and its possible cause and developed our goals:

> **Goal 1:** Create an easily memorizable five-option system by never altering fantasy between options and their interactions.
>
> **Goal 2:** Maintain the perfect balance of RPS, with each option having an equivalent number of win states and loss states.
>
> **Goal 3:** Ensure each hand gesture is easy to understand, is easily identifiable, and is distinguishable from the other gestures.

Now we need to maximize ideas. Before even attempting a brainstorm, we should look at the many examples of RPS that exist today. As mentioned earlier, David C. Lovelace created a 101-option RPS. He also created five-, seven-, nine-, eleven-, fifteen-, and twenty-five-option versions before moving on to 101. His five-option system exists in a flash game as *Rock, Paper, Scissors, Fire, Air:*

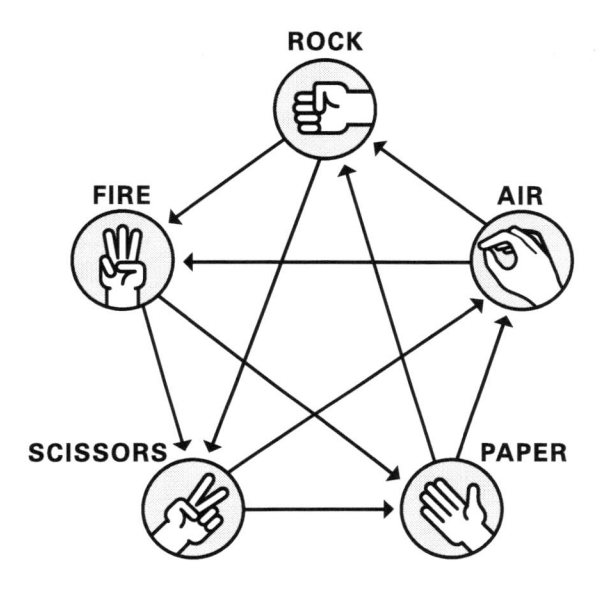

Fire burns Paper and melts Scissors but is smothered by Rock and blown out by Air.

Air blows out Fire and erodes Rock but is cut by Scissors and fanned by Paper.

Does this five-option system achieve our goals? Can we all go home now? The connections with Fire seem to work well, but Air brings up a new problem. Its interactions with Scissors and Fire seem reasonable. But Air eroding Rock? How many years does this interaction take? This also becomes a question of scale. A big-enough Rock actually blocks Air. Paper fans Air in this game, but wouldn't Paper be blown away by Air? The gust of Air needed to put out Fire or erode Rock would definitely send Paper flying. *Rock, Paper, Scissors, Fire, Air* has a similar yet different problem to the *Lizard-Spock* variant. Although the fantasy of each option doesn't change, the scale and complexity of the interactions do. This new problem forces us to create another goal:

Goal 4: All interactions must be simple enough to showcase with the revealed hand gestures; therefore, they must maintain the same scale.

Being able to showcase the victory with the revealed hand gestures ensures it's a simple, one-step interaction (Paper covers Rock). And since our hands never change scale, the interaction won't either.

Since our research didn't reveal any solutions that fit our needs, we must try to create our own. After researching all of Lovelace's 101-options, I was able to identify twenty-eight individual options that work with our goals and could be carried over into our brainstorm.

Brainstorm

We have defined the problem, hypothesized the cause, and developed our goals. Now we can offer up solutions. The main purpose of the brainstorm is to collect ideas that can solve the problem. The secondary purpose is to focus on our goals. The problem and goals should guide the brainstorm but not restrict anyone from thinking freely.

There are a few different ways to structure this specific brainstorm. Here are a few examples of where we could start:

- **Fantasy:** Brainstorm everyday objects that interact with Rock, Paper, and Scissors. This would lead to the most intuitive interactions.

- **Mechanics:** Brainstorm hand gestures that are easy to learn and obvious in their representation. This ensures intuitive hand gestures.

- **Interactions:** Brainstorm what could fit individual system requirements. For example, what beats Rock but loses to Paper and Scissors? This ensures the options can fit in the system, but they may be hard to tie to gestures.

- **System Structure:** Brainstorm the entire system structure and what it requires to be successful. This may be the toughest option to brainstorm, but it's closest in ensuring we have a perfect system at the end.

Some of these approaches may make perfect sense to you and others may seem crazy. But each of these brainstorms are completely valid. They simply use different perspectives to solve the problem and design the experience. I always prefer high-level systems discussions, so we'll move forward with the system structure option for this example.

System Structure Brainstorm

Trying to fit two more options into RPS yields three unique system configurations that could be valid. These are as follows:

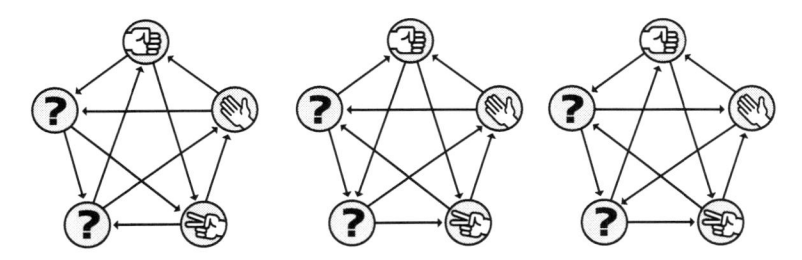

Notice how the lower left "?" beats two different RPS options in each scenario. This can be used as a great starting point for the brainstorm. For example, you might start with "What beats Rock and Scissors?" Here are the results of this type of brainstorm (done with friends):

Beats Rock & Scissors:
- Water
- Hammer
- Armor

- Wall
- Grenade
- Quicksand*

*Loses to Paper

Beats Paper & Scissors:
- Fire*
- Lightning*
- Gun
- Knife
- Gum

*Loses to Rock

Beats Rock & Paper:
- Hand*
- Claw*
- Dynamite*
- Weight
- Drill

*Loses to Scissors

Next, we compare all options marked with * to our goals. Many can be dropped due to our fourth goal requiring the interactions to maintain the same scale as the hand gestures. We have three options remaining: Fire, Claw, and Dynamite. Now we can focus on these options for our next round to solve for the second unknown "?"

Beats Fire & Rock
- Dirt
- Water
- Lava

*Loses to Paper & Scissors

Beats Claw & Scissors
- Hammer
- Metal
- Poop*

*Loses to Rock & Paper

Beats Dynamite & Scissors
- Poop*
- Shield
- Air

*Loses to Rock & Paper

After our brainstorms, it looks like we have two options: *Rock, Paper, Scissors, Claw, Poop* or *Rock, Paper, Scissors, Dynamite, Poop*. With two possible opportunities we can put aside brainstorming and move forward in the process.

Full disclosure: I decided to focus on the *Rock, Paper, Scissors, Lizard, Spock* problem while I was writing *Chapter 2: Defining Game Design.* I was stepping through the design process in real-time after writing each chapter on the process. For a while, my friends and I got stuck during the brainstorm and were unsure if we could solve the problem. And then Poop saved us! It was the missing link in the chain and reaffirmed what I have always believed: Every design problem has a solution.

CHAPTER 8

DESIGN THE SOLUTION

After analyzing other games/mediums, holding in-depth conversations on the problem, and brainstorming, you should have identified a few top ideas that might work out. Now it's time to expand these ideas into designs. As stated earlier, ideas can't be part of the game until turned into mechanics, systems, or rules. How can we know which idea is best before understanding how each one will be integrated into the game? Instinct? Because one sounds cooler? I've seen amazing ideas go to prototype that had major holes in how they interacted with other systems. These resulting prototypes can lead to weeks of wasted effort only to create bigger issues than they resolved. This step—designing the solution—is what separates game design from ideation. When you begin the process of designing solutions you should follow three steps.

1. **Ask yourself, "What problem am I trying to solve?"**
   Never forget that this is the number-one question to keep in mind when designing. It's surprisingly easy to lose sight of this goal and the other goals you've built.

2. **Understand the complexity of what you're thinking of adding to the game.** Is this idea a rule, mechanic, or system and how will it interact with the other rules, mechanics, and systems that already exist in the game?

    - New rules can end up clashing with existing rules or altering how mechanics and systems function.

    - New mechanics need to fit into existing systems and loops without creating holes. Make sure each connection makes sense, especially if a new mechanic is replacing an old mechanic.

    - New systems can do the most damage and generally require the most development time typically because they require a host of additional rules and mechanics to be added. All of these added rules and mechanics must work in harmony while bridging to existing systems in the game.

    - Again, the goal is to understand the idea's complexity and to identify the primary systems and mechanics the new design will interact with. Don't worry yet about all the secondary interactions that aren't related to the problem or your goals. It can take a while to fully design a feature and fill all the holes. We don't want to go too far until we've proven the main components of the design are successful via prototyping and testing.

3. **Design the gameplay experience in a quick, easily presentable format.** This is where we finally plan how fantasy, mechanics, rules, systems, challenge, and the player's goal all come together within our gameplay loops. Each designer will have their own approach in how to bring all of these together depending on their priorities and the focus of the game.

- Do you prefer to start with a focus on the player experience?
- Do you start with the emotions you want to push?
- How does this new design fit into the overall game structure or loops?
- What does it add to the long-term player goals?
- What challenges will the player use this design to overcome?

Every design must start somewhere. There is no wrong approach and the more we allow every designer to embrace their own perspective, the more success we'll see in the designs.

At the end of this process you should have a few basic designs that showcase how the top ideas solve the problem, achieve the goals, and successfully connect to the rest of the experience. Now it's time to share them with the team and get feedback. It's impossible to narrow in on an optimal solution without feedback. Gathering feedback generally works best in quick one-on-one discussions. After this, you'll pick the best option to prototype. There are many criteria that can be used to determine what "best" means for you. The following are a few things to consider:

> **Goals:** Which design best fits your goals? Which best solves the main problem? After fleshing out the design, you may realize that an idea doesn't align with your goals as you thought it would. Also, not all goals are created equal and some designs may do a better job at serving your higher-priority goals.
>
> **Fantasy:** Does the giant *Katamari*-style ball make no sense in your spy thriller game? At times, it makes

sense to bend your fantasy, but to break it means breaking immersion and the player experience. So, if your project takes its fantasy very seriously, then all your designs better match up.

Fun: "Fun" is an extremely subjective factor when picking a design, especially since it's all just paper design up to this point. And when we talk about "fun," we're not talking about it from your perspective but from that of your player. Earlier, we defined *fun* as "Exciting Fantasy/Mechanics + Challenging Systems/Goals." So which design will your players find more novel and exciting? Which design offers more opportunities to scale the challenge?

Scope: Is it possible to complete this feature in the time allowed? There's always some wiggle room with this calculation, and I find that if the team is extremely excited about a design then it's easier to push on scope a bit. That being said, I've met many designers who don't believe it's their job to think about scope. This mentality almost always ends up hurting the team. Scope shouldn't affect the brainstorm, but it should definitely affect the design picked to prototype.

Risk: How many other systems does this design affect? How many other areas may blow up because of this feature? Our goal as designers is to *solve* problems. Sometimes that means blowing things up so they can be rebuilt better. But if everything you touch keeps ending up with more problems, then you may not be following good design practices. Each design should solve problems and reduce the amount of issues in the game.

Development Cycle: How close are you to Alpha (feature complete), Beta (polished), or Shipping (bug free)? The dev cycle criteria are a combination of scope and risk. Beta is definitely not the time to blow up gameplay loops. And yet I've seen it done. There is one truth that can't be denied, if you're blowing things up late in the development cycle, then you're not actually late in the development cycle. You're early in the cycle facing either a deadline you're about to miss or a game that's going to ship with a ton of issues.

Taking into account these considerations, you should have a design that rises to the top of the pile as the most promising for solving the problem, achieving the goals, and fitting within the constraints of the project. If not, then rinse and repeat until you do.

Rock, Paper, Scissors, Lizard, Spock
Design the Solution

It's time to flesh out our five-option RPS designs based on the brainstorm results. We're adding two new mechanics to the system. We should double check our interactions and figure out the input and output of our mechanics.

In terms of interactions, the Claw throws Rock and slashes Paper but is stabbed by Scissors and flees from Poop (I would). The inputs are hand gestures. The Claw has a pretty straightforward hand gesture:

Dynamite blows up Rock and incinerates Paper, but its wick is cut by Scissors and it spreads Poop everywhere. Shoutout to Lovelace's 101-Option RPS which already has a good hand gesture with the thumb acting as the wick, although he has Dynamite beating Scissors and losing to Paper (I still don't understand that).

And now for Poop. Poop exists in both of our systems. In the Claw system, Poop ruins Scissors and scares the Claw, but Poop is covered by Rock and scooped by Paper. In our Dynamite system, Poop is spread by Dynamite and claims victory. Oddly enough, the thumbs up we use for Dynamite is somewhat similar to the ASL sign for Poop. So, let's just go with the poopiest hand signal we can come up with:

(palm down and knuckles flattened)

With our designs fleshed out, we are left with the following options:

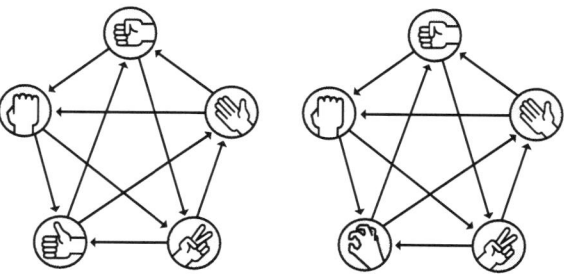

Rock, Paper, Scissors, Dynamite, Poop & Rock, Paper, Scissors, Claw, Poop

Design the Solution

In terms of fun, Dynamite could be considered a more exciting mechanic than Claw as it offers more novel interactions. Claw vs. Rock uses a similar interaction gesture as Paper vs. Rock, and it's always more exciting to blow things up. The only fantasy issue is that Dynamite sacrifices itself. It blows itself up to beat Rock and Scissors. This doesn't conflict with any of our goals so we will move forward and see if that issue comes up in testing.

The winner is Rock, Paper, Scissors, Dynamite, Poop due the novelty of Dynamite's interactions. We still have an acronym issue with two P's in RPSDP. It's a non-issue, but I will remain irked.

CHAPTER 9

PROTOTYPE THE SOLUTION

The goal of prototyping is to find the cheapest, most effective way to prove if the chosen design successfully solves the problem and creates a better overall gameplay experience. Prototypes can be developed in many ways. Here are a few common examples:

In Engine: If you're developing a video game, then building the prototype in the game engine is the most direct way to prove that the proposed solution actually solves the problem. But it can also be the most time-consuming approach or require an experienced programmer's time to implement. Therefore, it may not always be the optimal approach.

Paper Prototype: At times the cheapest option is to build a board game version of the solution. Board games are a good way to test gameplay systems with deep interactions among multiple players. And iteration can be as easy as using a pencil to alter a mechanic.

Logic Design: Nowadays there are many online programs that allow designers to develop and simulate complex systems in the form of logic design and gates. These types of programs are great for balancing large economies and running through complex simulations.

Game Reference: Showing examples in other games is a great resource when designing your experience. But we must always remember that any differences in your usage of that feature will most likely require a unique prototype to be built. For example, if you want to copy a boss attack used in another game, then you'll need a prototype unless your gameplay is identical in almost every way. Any difference in your weapons, movement, or health may create enough variance for that reference not to work. That being said, if you'll use the feature in the exact same way and in the same environment, then it's possible simply showing and playing the reference is sufficient to prove that it's a sound solution. Using game references as prototypes works especially well for industry standards.

No matter how you choose to build your prototype, its purpose is to prove it's a valid solution. This proof is achieved by testing the prototype before committing many more resources to fully building out the feature. All prototypes should be built with this test in mind to ensure that 100 percent of the time spent on the prototype is actually needed for the test. A major decision to make is whether your prototype will be tested by devs or by players outside the dev team:

Dev Prototype: This barebones prototype is the first to be achieved and allows the developers to determine if they are on a good path—first with how they are implementing the prototype and second with whether or not they should continue based on its success in solving the problem. This prototype needs almost no player-centric feedback as the developers know what is occurring. Many experienced developers may just use this when dealing with simple problems.

Playtest Prototype: This prototype will be tested by people outside the dev team. Therefore, it needs appropriate signs and feedback for external players to understand the experience and successfully complete the playtest. *Signs* are signals that reveal the capabilities (or affordance) of a feature before the player takes action. Examples include UI prompts to pick up objects or the understanding that a character holding a gun can shoot. *Feedback* appears after the player has taken action and helps the player understand what the action accomplished. This feedback may be visual, audio, or tactile such as a controller rumble, the muzzle flash of a gun, or a bullet decal when a shot hits a wall. Signs and feedback help the player discover the feature, understand its use, and utilize it successfully in the gameplay experience. If players don't understand your features during a playtest, they'll have a negative experience and you'll have trouble determining whether your solutions are working.

If the prototype will be seen by others, the designer will need to think about the user experience. User experience, or UX, is commonly confused with user interface, or UI. User experience encompasses the user's *entire* experience with the product, from first exposure to the end of the product's lifecycle. User interface, on the other hand, is a small component of UX, and may refer, for example, to the menu systems within the product itself.

When it comes to UX, the first time that consumers see an advertisement they begin to develop expectations. These expectations impact if and how they use the product. And even after they stop using the product, the brand may continue to develop updates and addons and try to market them to the consumer through emails and ads. The UX relationship between the consumer and the product may go on for the rest of the consumer's life. I know, for example, that my relationship with Wendy's is never-ending. However, for the sake of simplicity, let's say the portion of UX owned by game designers begins when the game is turned on and ends when it is turned off.

When designing and building the UX for a prototype, the designer must ask two major questions:

- How will the player discover the feature?
- How will the player understand the feature?

Without those answers built into the design, the playtester will spend most of their time ignoring or misunderstanding the feature instead of demonstrating whether or not it solves the problem. A prototype with poor UX can lead to an unsuccessful test result even if the prototype does successfully solve the problem.

To learn more about UX design, I highly recommend the book *The Design of Everyday Things* by one of the forefathers of UX, Don Norman.

The prototype phase ends when you have a minimal prototype ready that you believe solves the problem, speaks to each of your goals, and has an appropriate UX in order for it to be tested.

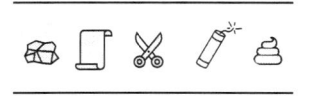

Rock, Paper, Scissors, Dynamite, Poop
Prototype the Solution

As I mentioned before, designers should understand how they'll determine the success of a prototype before building it. The prototype should be built with the test in mind to help reduce the prototype's requirements to a minimum. Looking back at our goals for *Rock, Paper, Scissors, Dynamite, Poop* we can come up with a few questions for our test to figure out:

- Are the new hand gestures memorable and intuitive?
- Are the new interactions memorable and intuitive?
- Are the new elements positive additions to the RPS experience? (This Appreciation question is almost always needed.)

To answer these questions, we'll want to run external playtests with participants who have played RPS before but are completely new to RPSDP. If we find that no players are using the new options, we may need to shorten the game to *Rock, Dynamite, Poop* to help test if the hand gestures are intuitive and go from there.

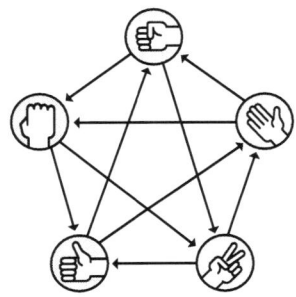

Rock, Paper, Scissors, Dynamite, Poop

The Role of a Great Game Designer

Due to the nature of RPS, our prototype is already built. The mechanics are hand gestures and the system is a memorized list of interactions. The exciting revelation is that if this exact experience were going to be made into a video game, the developers could use a simple hand gesture prototype to prove it out before committing to building it virtually. Hand gestures, dice, and board games are all valid ways to prototype mechanics and systems before building them into a video game.

Of course, we also have the following UX questions:

- How will the player discover the feature?
- How will the player understand the feature?

The player will be told of the new features, their gestures, and their interactions before playing. The real test is whether they can quickly and easily recall this information while playing.

Throughout this entire process it's important to keep one thing in mind: Don't be afraid to fail.

CHAPTER 10

PLAYTEST THE SOLUTION

Of all the phases in the design process, testing can be the most complicated piece. I will oversimplify it for the purpose of this book. If you wish to get a sense of the full scope of user research testing for game development, I highly recommend the book *Games User Research* by Anders Drachen, Pejman Mirza-Babaei, and Lennart Nacke.

In terms of our scientific approach to design, playtests are experiments that test our hypothesized cause of the problem by verifying if our solution solved the problem. The questions we need answered in this test are as follows:

- Was the problem solved?
- Were our goals achieved?
- Did our key performance indicator (appreciation, retention, etc.) increase?

You can ask many other questions, but these are the most important to validate your designs. When you are setting up the test, you should also ask, "What datapoints can I collect that will help find the answers to those three important questions?" Every decision about the playtest setup should be driven toward getting that data.

Test Type

Many different forms of testing exist, and each one has its own pros and cons depending on the questions you need answered. Here are a few examples:

> **Usability testing** focuses on finding issues with the player's ability to understand the experience. This form of testing generally requires a one-on-one approach with the participant. Being more hands-on allows the playtest manager to direct the participant, pick up on any frustrations during the session, and ask questions as they play. This approach won't give you a large amount of data for tracking trends.
>
> **A/B testing** helps you decide between two options by pushing both to separate consumer groups and testing performance. This type of testing is the preferred approach for most live titles. It also requires a key performance indicator (KPI) that you'll track to determine which option is more successful. This approach needs a large number of users in order for the KPI to showcase meaningful and valid results.
>
> **Appreciation testing** asks groups of gamers to score their appreciation of the experience after they play. This allows you to track appreciation for one session as well as over multiple sessions as more features are added to the build. If scores dip between tests you'll (hopefully) be able to track down the reason for the dip and resolve it. This approach requires frequent testing to minimize the feature delta between each test.

The list of testing formats goes on and on. No matter what you're looking for, there's most likely a test for you. The most important piece is knowing what you need answered.

Participants

The participants you'll test are as important as the test itself. You'll want to find players who are close to your intended market. To do so you'll gather demographic information like their age, gaming habits, and preferred genre. Here is a list of participants you can utilize along with their best use.

Yourself: This is usually the go-to option for many designers. It's fine to be your first option as you need to play the experience in order to tell if it's ready to test, but it should definitely not be your only option. You are, by far, the most biased user when testing your own features.

Dev Team: Fellow developers on the team are easy users to access and can offer great feedback. But they also have a lot of inside knowledge on the experience and can come with a jaded perspective as they may already be for or against the chosen design. Most prototype playtests are done with the dev team. This is due to the simple fact that time and money are always limited so it's not practical to run larger playtests for every feature.

Internal Playtesters: These are other employees at your studio or company. They know less about your project, your goals, and what you're specifically trying to test. But they can still be biased as they may feel your project is competing with theirs or they may want to join your team. It's also hard for fellow developers to get in the headspace of a regular player while still at the office.

External Playtesters: These are average consumers from outside the industry who have agreed to help you test your game. They are a great option for unbiased feedback, but it can be difficult to ensure they are within your target market. The honest truth is that if they won't buy your game when it releases, then they aren't your actual consumers. And if they aren't, how much should you alter your game based on their feedback? These candidates are great at revealing problems, but it's up to you to determine if the problems are important enough to be fixed.

Live Players: These, in my opinion, are the only truly unbiased participants, players who have actively installed your game and are playing on their own time. They are the only ones sacrificing their time and money to play your experience. They are also the only players on the list who are 100 percent your consumers and target market. The sooner you can get your game into their hands for testing the better. This could mean using early access or open betas, for example.

This list goes from the most biased to least biased option in terms of feedback and data. It also goes from the least expensive and time-consuming option to the highest-cost option. As with everything else, choosing your final test group is a balancing act. In my experience, the more important the feature is in determining the success of your product, the further down this list you should be in terms of test participants.

Gathering Data

There's no point to a playtest unless you gather data you can use to answer your test questions. This data can be gathered in the following ways:

Dev Discussions: Many prototypes won't go through rigorous testing. Instead, the developers will play and draw their own conclusions. It's still important to have an open discussion on everyone's experiences with the prototype. Such a discussion can lead to important findings that would otherwise be missed. Also make sure you grab some developers who didn't work on the specific feature in question.

Observation: When it comes to identifying user experience and qualitative issues, observe the people playing your game. Witnessing the play first-hand, whether from behind glass or via a live stream, gives you instant information on the successes and failures of the experience. That being said, raw observations can be misinterpreted so it's best to pair this strategy with another data point to validate your assumptions.

Surveys: Having each participant fill out a questionnaire or provide verbal feedback allows you to collect qualitative data. Doing this on a five-point Likert Scale (Strongly Disagree → Strongly Agree) allows you to collect it in a quantitative manner so it can be more easily tracked across multiple tests. The trick is asking each question in an objective way so as not to influence the playtest answers.

Telemetry: Telemetry requires building triggers into the game itself that will send data to a server from where it can be referenced later. Telemetry is an absolute requirement for fine-tuning weapon balance, map balance, and progression systems. Before adding a ton of these triggers, always make sure you know how you'll use the data. Flooding your database with data you don't need will just add confusion. It's usually best to set up data tables and graphs to prove out the need and then use those same formats later to study the data. These data hooks are extremely important post-launch to identify player patterns and issues. Getting them in for playtests will not only help you identify player patterns early but will also test out your telemetry pipeline for later.

With all of the above figured out, it's time to run your playtest and collect your data.

Rock, Paper, Scissors, Dynamite, Poop
Test the Solution

With our prototype ready, it's time to test *Rock, Paper, Scissors, Dynamite, Poop* (RPSDP). As a reminder, these are the questions we need our test to answer:

- Are the new hand gestures memorable and intuitive?
- Are the new interactions memorable and intuitive?
- Are the new elements positive additions to the RPS experience? (This Appreciation question is almost always needed.)

Based on the questions we need answered, we'll go for a usability test. This one-on-one approach with the participant allows the playtest manager to pick up on any frustrations during the session, and ask questions as they play. Also, in order to understand if our *Rock, Paper, Scissors, Dynamite, Poop* interactions are more intuitive, we'll run the same test on *Rock, Paper, Scissors, Lizard, Spock* (RPSLS).

Test Type: Usability study with five players

Participants: External playtesters aged 18–34 who have played RPS

Gathering Data: Observation and surveys

RPSDP Test Flow. Our playtest manager will observe five individual participants while also acting as their competitor. Usually you wouldn't want to include the playtest manager in the test itself. But ensuring we only have one test participant at a time also ensures the outcome isn't swayed by a loud personality who speaks for both players. To mitigate any issues with the playtest manager being the competitor, the playtest manager will throw the same consecutive hand gestures against all participants.

The playtest manager will explain the rules of *Rock, Paper, Scissors, Dynamite, Poop* by showing each option and explaining what it beats. Afterward, the manager and the playtester will play ten matches of RPSDP. The participant will be expected to play and explain who they believe won each match. The playtest manager will not guide the players in any way or answer questions about the game's mechanics or interactions. The manager will observe and record all options thrown along with the option determined to be the winner.

After all ten matches are complete, the manager will ask the following and take notes on the answers:

- How was the experience?
- What are your thoughts about the two new options?
- What are your thoughts about the new interactions?

In order to test the full comprehension of the RPSDP conceptual model, the final question will showcase a model of the options and ask the player to name each option and draw lines to showcase the appropriate interactions.

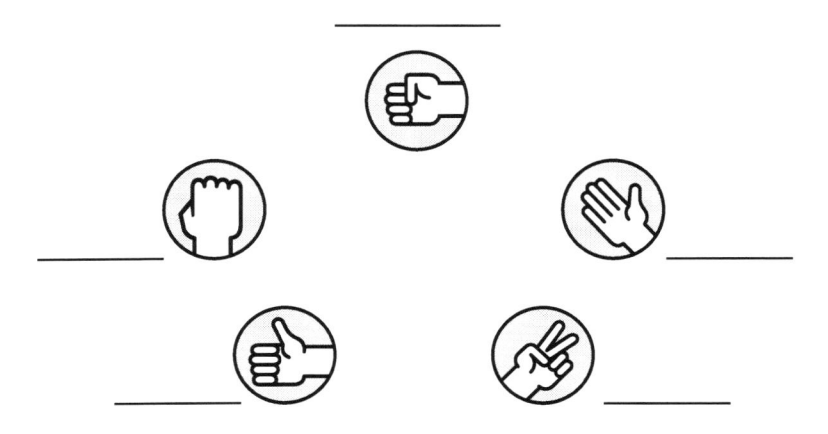

RPSDP: Blank Conceptual Model

RPSLS Test Flow. The *Rock, Paper, Scissors, Lizard, Spock* playtest will use a different set of five participants and utilize the same flow and survey questions described for RPSDP. No participants may have played or heard of RPSLS before.

After all testing is complete, we'll compile the data for analysis.

CHAPTER 11

ANALYZE PLAYTEST RESULTS

Once you have all your playtest data, it's time to examine it and identify patterns. When studying data, we should put all our assumptions aside. Do not go in trying to validate preconceived notions or looking for data you agree with. The best way to approach this is to already have an unbiased plan for how to sort through each datapoint.

Gaining experience in analyzing data will help you build better questions and data requests for future playtests. With better data you can ensure you're getting everything you need to identify problems and their causes and determine if they need a solution.

Observations

Observations can be one of the easiest forms of data to interpret incorrectly due to biases. Although observation is still a useful tool, we must be aware that what we witness may be deceiving or raise more questions than it answers:

> The players *seemed* frustrated with a puzzle. They took a lot longer than expected to complete it. But they were also pumped when they finally solved it. Should we reduce the possible frustrations or did those frustrations help to increase the payoff? Were they frustrated with the game or with themselves? Do they blame the game, or are they hoping to increase their skills to reduce future frustrations?

It's important to watch participants playing our games. It can help us better understand the major pain points and successes. But it's also important to have other datapoints that can validate our observations. Without these datapoints, we'll end up making a lot of assumptions and possibly draw the wrong conclusions.

If observations raise more questions, then we'll need to get answers before we can understand if there is a problem to solve. Many of these answers can be obtained directly from the participant via surveys.

Surveys

Each survey question should offer data you can use to validate the playtest goals and determine your successes or failures. In my experience, pairing Likert Scale questions with an opportunity for open comments is a good approach to hone in on specific issues and track progress over the entire development cycle. Although one test can offer good insights, comparing that data from test to test will show if you're on the right track or not. For example, you should notice that appreciation is increasing.

Likert Scale (Five Options)

How satisfied are you with the weapon variety?

[Chart showing line graph with values: Very Unsatisfied: 0, Unsatisfied: 3, Neutral: 7, Satisfied: 8, Very Satisfied: 4]

The Likert Scale can showcase where you currently stand with your players; their comments will help you understand *why* they feel the way they do. This will get you closer to understanding the actual problem:

> **Player 3** (Neutral): "I understand these maps are smaller but I still want a sniper rifle."
>
> **Player 4** (Satisfied): "I only use assault rifles in games like these. They feel great."
>
> **Player 9** (Unsatisfied): "Pistols seem useless."
>
> **Average Score:** 3.6/5

After analyzing this type of data, a designer still must determine the root cause of any problems and whether solving a problem is in conflict with the vision. For example, the entire game may not support maps big enough to justify adding a sniper rifle, but there may be an opportunity that allows for a powerful precision-based weapon that doesn't need long sightlines.

From these types of charts, it can be hard to draw conclusions unless you have player comments and charts from previous playtests to compare. That being said, if most players gave a game a one out of five, you can more easily draw the conclusion that something is horribly wrong (or right, depending on how you worded the question).

Telemetry

Telemetry is an amazing tool when implemented well and completely daunting when used poorly. Having many telemetry hooks will always seem like a great idea until you look at the mountain of data that was collected.

Here are a few best practices, most of which were found out the hard way:

Always on

Many teams will default their telemetry collection to Off to ensure they don't have a database filled with garbage data from the dev team. But we found this approach always led to missed opportunities as it required someone to remember to turn it on each time. Almost every project I've seen start this way ends up leaving it on in the end and using filters to find the appropriate data through session ID, timestamp, or other useful datapoints (i.e., number of players). Also, database space is usually not an issue nowadays.

Another reason to leave telemetry on for the dev team is that the data can still be useful. For example, you may find that 90 percent of dev team weapon kills are done with the default weapon when dev-spawning into a map. This means that 90 percent of all testing and feedback from the team is focused on one weapon. A situation like this led to creating a loadout randomizer for *Starlink: Battle for Atlas* (Ubisoft, 2018) to ensure the team was trying out new combinations all the time. On *Dead Space,* the dev team used the Plasma Cutter weapon throughout development. This ensured the Plasma Cutter felt great, but it also led to our players using the Plasma Cutter almost exclusively throughout the game. The other weapons weren't up to par.

Naming Conventions

Agree on solid datapoint naming conventions so everyone knows what they're looking at. This may seem obvious but it gets more complicated when you want to track the weapon Player A killed Player B with and the weapon Player B held while dying. It's best if your names are close to the action that triggered the data: Weapon_Kill and Weapon_OnDeath. It's also useful to create a legend on an internal wiki page that everyone can access.

Rigorous Testing

Test your telemetry to validate its correctness. If the data are wrong in any way, whether due to lost packets or incorrect calculations, then they will be useless.

Know How You'll Use It

All of these points are important, but this one may be the most important. Many designers have a tendency to ask for a lot of datapoints they never end up using. They may feel that a reason will come up later and they'll be happy they had the data. Or they may have a question they want to answer like "How effective is this weapon?" but be unsure how to answer it, so they'll ask for all related datapoints. This design approach can lead to wasted engineering effort, messy databases, and wordy naming conventions to distinguish so many random types of data.

To get ahead of this, designers should understand what they need to prove the success of each design. This means not only going after the right data points, but also structuring the tables and graphs they plan on filling. They should also determine a successful metric they hope to see in those charts. Example charts for weapon effectiveness, for example, could include weapon accuracy, kill range, damage per second, and weapon showdown stats (regarding which weapon statistically wins in a one-on-one fight).

The Analysis

When analyzing *qualitative* data, you're looking for common thoughts and feelings shared by a good percentage of your participants. You're also looking for correlations between feedback and gameplay success. Players who win are more likely to leave positive feedback than are players who lose.

When analyzing *quantitative* data, you should already have an idea of the target numbers you're looking for:

- Are you expecting an equal use of weapon types across all players in a match?
- Does that change based on the map played?
- What types of usage numbers would raise a red flag that one weapon type may be too powerful?

Having design intentions and an idea of industry expectations will help you interpret the data. And remember that almost all your effort in analyzing the data should be directed to finding the answers to these questions:

- Was the problem solved?
- Were our goals achieved?
- Did our key performance indicator (appreciation, retention, etc.) increase?

Always keep an eye out for new problems that may have been caused by the prototype.

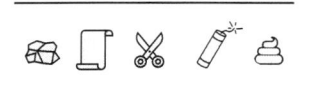

Rock, Paper, Scissors, Dynamite, Poop
Analyze Data

We have successfully playtested RPSDP and RPSLS with usability testing. Our data were collected by running tests on random people hanging out at a local park. All participants were tested individually. Participants completed ten matches against the playtest manager and were asked to determine the victor of each match. They were then asked to answer the following questions and fill out the conceptual model:

- How was the experience?
- What are your thoughts on the two new options?
- What are your thoughts on the new interactions?

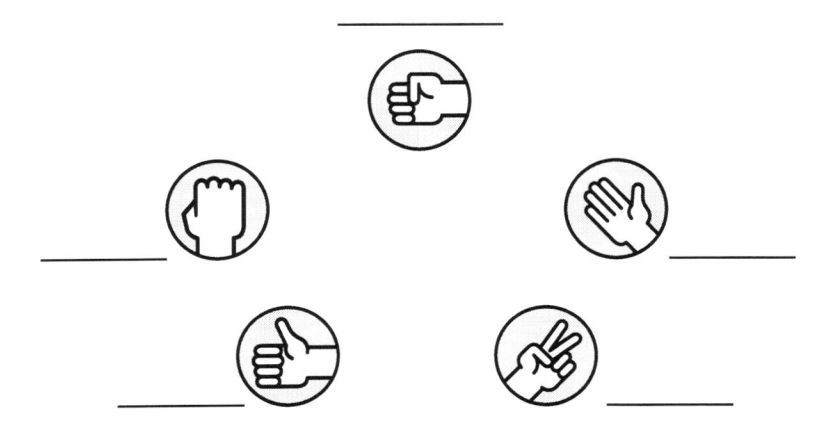

RPSDP: Blank Conceptual Model

This test was completed with five participants for RPSDP (Participants A–E) and five different participants for RPSLS (Participants F–J).

RPSDP Playtest Data. Of the five participants tested, four went through all ten matches without issues. One participant (Participant B) determined the wrong winner of one match by declaring that Rock beat Dynamite.

Comment Highlights. Participants provided positive comments on the overall experience with the exception of Participant D who considered it "A bit juvenile." Three other participants considered the experience to be funnier, more fun, and more interesting than the standard RPS experience.

Conceptual Model. All participants correctly detailed the conceptual model except for Participant B who had Rock beating Dynamite.

Summary. Overall, the Dynamite and Poop hand gestures and interactions can be considered intuitive based on the results of this test. It can be expected that in a live environment, the opposing player would clear up the confusion Participant B had with Rock vs. Dynamite.

RPSLS Playtest Data. Of the five participants tested, only one participant went through all ten matches without issues. The remaining four participants (Participants F, H, I, J) incorrectly identified that Spock beat Lizard, some on multiple occasions. Participant H also incorrectly declared that Scissors beat Spock.

Comment Highlights. Comments were mixed on the overall experience, with two participants confirming they were confused about interactions with Spock. One participant mentioned that they had trouble making the Spock hand gesture.

Conceptual Model. Many participants detailed the conceptual models incorrectly, believing Spock beat Lizard. Two participants, understanding that each option should win two and lose two, spent a long time correcting their conceptual models.

Summary. The Spock and Lizard additions to RPS came with multiple usability concerns. It can be concluded that the interaction between Spock and Lizard is not intuitive. Also, there may be accessibility issues with the Spock hand gesture.

CHAPTER 12

FINALIZE OR ITERATE

We've reached the last stage of the process. At this stage, there are two possible outcomes:

> **Problem Not Solved**: The problem isn't fixed or you've created bigger issues. Don't be discouraged. It's time to try again. The secret to success with an iterative, creative process is to be open to failing. As long as you learned something, it can still be considered a gain. That added knowledge will help you arrive at a better solution on your next attempt.
>
> **Problem Solved**: The problem is solved or reduced enough that you're satisfied with the progress. It's just a prototype so there's a lot more work to do, but you know this direction will take you there. You can now finalize the design and embark on the journey to full implementation of the feature.

This process may seem to involve a lot of steps, but each of these steps is necessary to ensure the design is moving toward the vision and a shippable product. The full design process from beginning to end for a developer-playtested prototype may only take a few days depending on the feature.

Iterate (Problem Not Solved)

The design process is not a perfect loop. When you reach this point and need to iterate, there are still many possible avenues to take. You could end up going back to any step in the design process based on the situation:

> **Identify the Problem:** The solution worked exactly as you expected and fixed the issue you thought was causing the problem. But the problem still persists. Now you need to jump back to the first step and re-evaluate what the true cause of the problem could be.
>
> **Build Goals**: The solution may have worked but the experience is veering away from your vision. Or you need new ideas but want to refine your goals first to ensure the next design better fits the bill.
>
> **Maximize Ideas**: The cause you identified wasn't resolved with your prototype and you aren't confident in the other designs you have. Time to gather more ideas.
>
> **Design the Solution:** The design you prototyped didn't work out but you have others to try. Instead of rushing in with one of the other designs, it's best to take the knowledge gained from the failed prototype and use it to strengthen the other designs.
>
> **Prototype the Solution**: You may have been on the right track but need to refine your prototype and try again. As long as you keep your goals in mind, iterating on a prototype can be a lot more fruitful than restarting with a new idea.
>
> **Playtest the Solution:** The data you obtained wasn't the data you needed to prove the design intentions. Or the playtest was faulty due to incorrect procedure or testing the wrong participants.

Analyze Playtest Results: The analysis was done incorrectly. This could be due to having too much bias while looking through the data, utilizing the data in the wrong way, or having so much data that it was hard to compile. In any of these cases, it's always good to get a second set of eyes to help you sort through the problem.

Knowing the right step to jump back to is crucial. I've seen teams waste time going through redesign after redesign when the real problem was with their goals. If there is ever any doubt, hold a quick post-mortem with the developers involved to discuss the options.

Finalize (Problem Solved)

Congrats on solving the problem and proving out a better gameplay experience. Don't get too comfortable though. You've proven this solution will work, but now it's time to flesh out the full design. This includes expanding on the following:

- Connections to all other rules/mechanics/systems
- Player discoverability and understanding (onboarding, signs, feedback)
- User interface requirements
- Full asset list (art, animation, audio)
- Dev tools (testing, tuning)
- Development milestone requirements (alpha complete, polished, etc.)

You are now the owner for this feature. You must track its progress throughout development and stay up-to-date with its latest status. You must keep the feature in a playable state no matter what other features are broken or coming down the pipe. When the feature has hit a milestone, you're the person who will push for reviews and additional playtests. When it's at risk, you're the one who must raise the red flag. Always keep a positive, collaborative dialogue with all devs who touch this feature. Also, play the game every day to keep up with how this feature is impacting the overall experience.

Be open to all feedback from the team and maintain an updated list of improvement ideas. This feature will most likely run into more issues as the full design is developed, as other features are added, and as you run playtests for feedback. When that happens, you'll need to re-enter this design process to identify and solve the new problems.

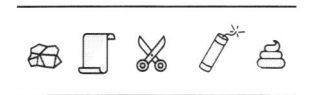

Rock, Paper, Scissors, Dynamite, Poop

Finalize or Iterate

After analyzing the RPSDP playtest data, we can safely say that we created a successful solution to the problem and a fun alternative to standard RPS. The novelty of the interactions with Dynamite and Poop was considered funny and fun, although the game may not be for all audiences.

Team Effort

This game design process may seem like a lot, but smaller features may only take a few days from beginning to end. Larger features and key differentiators could take weeks or possibly months. But that's the job.

Every step of the process is a team effort. Team involvement at every level is the difference between someone who designs games and a true game designer. We are leaders who must drive the gameplay experience by utilizing the team, not by dictating. One mind alone is too limited and one voice is too small. Infinite design opportunities exist for any given problem. To believe that any individual can come up with the best ideas that lead to the greatest designs is not only misguided; it's also a bit arrogant. It's unlikely for that one mind even to get in the ballpark of the top one million ideas that could lead to the top ten thousand designs. And no matter what that one person comes up with, they will 100 percent believe it's great unless someone else is there for a reality check.

We must drive to push the feeling of ownership into the team. If the team feels ownership in the design, then they'll be there for the product. Have you ever witnessed a team so demoralized and stepped over that they just start leaving the studio mid-milestone? Or a team that has completely lost faith in the designer? The gameplay experience is at the heart of the game, and the game designer is at the heart of the gameplay experience. Much of a team's morale and passion depends on the design culture of that team. An effective culture requires game designers to be solid leaders and listeners. They need to inspire and be open to ideas and feedback. If not, everything starts to spiral downward.

This is why the skills and capabilities of every game designer must go beyond game design.

PART THREE

● ● ●

SKILLS

CHAPTER 13

CORE SKILLS

Building a solid vision and driving a successful design process are great challenges, and most designers focus on developing skills in these areas. But the toughest challenge is getting the entire team to believe in that vision, follow it, and feel ownership of the features that are designed. Many designers don't prioritize this part of the role and therefore don't develop the skills to manage these challenges. As I advanced through my career, my responsibilities shifted towards managing, mentoring, and helping to diagnose design issues on other projects. All of these tasks required me to develop and continue refining a list of core skills that all game designers need in order to succeed.

When it comes to game designer skills, I've found there are two major categories:

> **Core Skills:** The hard and soft skills required to own the vision for the gameplay experience, drive the design process, and lead features throughout development. These skills are required by all game designers.

Specialty Skills: More advanced skills that will differ among design specialties (gameplay, AI, progression, etc.). These skill requirements may also differ from team to team based on a project's needs. A comprehensive list of specialty skills is outside the scope of this book but something that should be determined at each studio.

Most companies institute an annual performance review process in which managers formally review the skills of their direct reports. But without a strong, defined list of core skills, most of these processes end with vague outcomes like "Work on your soft skills." In order to help designers increase their skills year after year, we need to get more specific about which skills need work. This realization led me to the creation of the following chapters.

The next chapters represent a deep dive into the core skills required of every game designer. I'll go through the basics expected of junior to intermediate designers and then through the advanced versions of each skill that I expect from seniors and higher. Finally, I wrap up each skill with accessible methods for designers to increase their abilities in that skill. The core skills are the foundation of every game designer. In my opinion, struggling with any one of these skills can hold back a designer's career progression. But it's also on the manager to facilitate skill growth and continued success.

Core Hard Skills

- Developing a vision
- Conceiving rules, mechanics, & systems
- Creative problem solving
- Prototyping & in-engine development
- Analyzing the market

Core Soft Skills

- Driving the gameplay experience
- Collaborative design
- Pitching & selling

CHAPTER 14

CORE HARD SKILLS

When it comes to hard skills we generally think of technical skills like programming. The technical aspects for game designers are related to vision creation, designing mechanics and systems, building prototypes, and even analyzing other experiences.

This chapter will discuss each core hard skill, the competencies expected of junior to senior designers, and ways to develop each skill further. The following hard skills are needed by every game designer in the industry:

- Developing a vision
- Conceiving rules, mechanics, & systems
- Creative problem solving
- Prototyping & in-engine development
- Analyzing the market

Developing a Vision

Game designers drive the gameplay experience from start to finish. That experience must start with a gameplay vision: an understanding of how all their systems will come together into a cohesive experience. Without that vision, their designs will have no unified purpose and ideas will be picked purely based on subjective whims. Without a vision, the development will have no aims and endlessly wander, looking for something interesting to cling to. This unstructured approach may be somewhat okay for a sole developer, but the moment you add a team, the frustrations start to build. The gameplay vision must be built and owned by the entire design team, while being open to feedback from the entire development team.

Basics

Junior and intermediate designers will focus on developing the gameplay vision for individual features and ensuring it connects to the mid-level and high-level visions. Succeeding at the following abilities will showcase your skills in this area and determine whether you're ready for a bigger mandate.

Build Low-Level Vision. Low-level vision equates to the goals that drive each feature and the feature's connections to the systems around it. Building a feature's vision should always start with an understanding of what problem the feature is trying to solve. The designer must also understand the goals for the overall game, the gameplay experience, and their gameplay specialty (AI, progression, etc.). The designer must then build goals for the individual mechanics and systems while ensuring perfect alignment with the game's other goals. Conflicts will arise if a feature's goals conflict with any high-level project goals.

Developing feature goals is one of the most important steps before diving into a design or prototype. Without knowing what you're trying to solve or hoping to achieve, you'll just be throwing spaghetti at the wall. Also, if your goals don't inspire, then your feature won't inspire. Solid goals lead to solid features.

Understand Game/Gameplay Loops. Objective > Challenge > Reward loops are the building blocks of the gameplay experience and the player's motivation. They force designers to ask the basic question, "What drives players to use this feature?" Building features that aren't tied to these loops will lead to experiences that players aren't driven to play. Floating features don't add to the core gameplay experience and end up as confusing one-off toys. Every gameplay feature should be part of a gameplay loop and preferably the core gameplay loop that players will be engaged in for a majority of the experience. It's on game designers to understand their loops and how they function in order to evaluate their features.

Focusing on each individual beat of a gameplay loop can help designers focus their feature set. This focus can reveal new ways to increase or decrease the challenge for players. For example, *Dead Space* had a unique gameplay loop to take down necromorphs: Target > Fire > Dismember. Features like stasis were used to lessen the challenge of target, while many necromorph's limbs and animations were designed to increase that challenge. This loop contained the game's differentiator. As a result, a majority of the game's mechanics focused on this loop.

Advanced

Senior designers will focus on developing mid-level gameplay vision for entire design specializations (AI, combat, progression, etc.) or high-level gameplay vision for the entire gameplay experience. Success in these areas means there will be an aligned team that will march in the same direction. Failure means confusion, lost effort, and usually a lot of redesign.

Build Mid-level Vision. Mid-level gameplay vision focuses on an entire specialization within the gameplay experience. It translates the high-level vision toward that specialty and creates goals that bring all features within that specialty together.

The user interface of Dead Space had the goal of never breaking the fourth wall, which derived from the game's vision of building a completely immersive horror experience. The goal of never breaking the fourth wall went into everything we did on the UI team. At the time, it was a groundbreaking goal that created a truly memorable experience. But, in reality, it was just a simple goal built off another simple game vision. Innovation doesn't need to be complex and usually isn't. Building a solid mid-level vision means pushing simple, easy to understand goals that will elevate the vision for the overall game and strengthen the impact your specialty will have on the entire experience.

Build High-Level Vision. The high-level gameplay vision summarizes the entire gameplay experience. It doesn't focus on individual features and is therefore a harder concept to grasp for many first-time owners. Directors without this skill will tend to push many mid-level visions and even low-level visions instead of one unified high-level vision.

This vision requires broader concepts and player verbs that all design specialties can use to develop their experiences. It ensures everyone is speaking the same language, allowing them to develop the experience further. This vision focuses on the feeling that the experience is aiming at or the overall goals the experience is trying to achieve. For example, the *Dead Space* gameplay experience wanted players to feel tense and claustrophobic. So when *Dead Space 3* went planetside and made wider hallways for co-op, some players mentioned the experience felt less *Dead Space.* High-level vision can become subtle as it's translated into all specializations, but it's nevertheless felt throughout the entire experience.

How to Develop Vision Skills

Vision may seem really complex but that's mostly because I'm focusing on AAA games in my examples. On those large titles, the ownership of the vision is shared across many game designers. Developing visions for smaller titles is much simpler. Developing your skills in building vision may be more easily accomplished by analyzing smaller titles with fewer features.

Analyze Goals. Goals are related to the problems you're trying to solve or the intentions you have with the experience. Sometimes your goals will become more developed as you design a feature. Study features you designed in the past and ask yourself these questions:

- Why did I design it this way?
- What problem was I trying to solve?

Once you are able to answer those questions more easily, turn to features in games you didn't design and try to discern the goals the designers had when developing their features. You might not be able to get it exactly right but you can get pretty close.

This exercise is especially useful when you find a frustrating mechanic in a game. Take it further. Try to figure out why it was designed that way. Don't assume it's because of a bad designer. You'll usually find their reasoning as you study their other mechanics and systems.

Break Down Loops. Analyze your favorite games and determine the gameplay loops that drive their gameplay experience.

The simplest way to do this is to start with the game's main objective. Then determine what actions you enact to complete that objective. You'll always find patterns, things you do on repeat. Dive deeper into those activities to study the base actions that allow a player to progress and drive the player to keep playing. After you have an idea of the loops, look into all the features and mechanics that enhance those loops. If you're not feeling hooked by the loops, dive deeper to figure out why and how you would resolve that issue.

Conceiving Rules, Mechanics, and Systems

As game designers, we create interactive worlds. We develop the rules for how a world works as well as the systems for how it behaves and the mechanics players use to interact with it all. Anyone can throw ideas at a game. A game designer's job is to transform ideas into rules, mechanics, and systems that develop into the desired experience, preferably without holes or conflicts.

Basics

Most junior designers come in thinking their role is about ideation. They are usually surprised at how much systems design goes into making sure a door works without breaking the entire player experience. As a junior to mid-level game designer, you should be focused on the following concerns.

Build Intuitive Mechanics. The simplest parts of how a world functions can be deceptively difficult to design. For example, picking up an item is a simple task in the real world, but in a game there are numerous design questions that ensure the mechanic is intuitive and not frustrating:

- How can the player tell the item can be picked up?
- How close does the player's avatar need to be?
- Does the player's camera need to be looking at the item? Is the ability to pick up just based on proximity? Both camera and proximity?
- What happens when multiple items are near each other? Which takes priority?
- Is a button press required or is the item automatically picked up? If a button, which button? How will the player know the button?
- Do the avatar's hands animate to the item or does the item just disappear?
- Are there audio cues on pickup? Is there a message on the heads-up display (HUD)?
- Where does the item go after it is picked up? In the avatar's hands? In their inventory? How will the player know?
- What happens if the player's inventory is full? How will the player know they can't pick up the item?

All of this complexity exists, and we haven't even begun to design what the player can do with the item after acquiring it (throw, use, sell, dismantle, upgrade, craft, etc.). As a designer, you must break down every aspect of a mechanic in order to ensure not only its comfort and intuitiveness, but also consistent results.

Balance Systems. When it comes to systems design, there are many forms of balance and they generally revolve around fairness and maintaining a positive experience. In games and in life, nobody likes to feel cheated. In games and not in life, players want to overcome challenging experiences instead of walking through unchallenged. The following are a few forms of systems balance you'll encounter as a game designer:

Competitive balance is the hardest form to achieve. A system like RPS is fair because there are equal opportunities to win or lose. In systems based on skill, players need to feel that their victories were earned, and even more important, they must feel their losses were earned either by underperforming or by being outperformed by an opponent. Without this information readily available, players may blame the game's balance or call their opponents cheaters even if no issues really exist.

Effort vs. reward is a form of balance found in all gameplay experiences. The goal is for players to feel that their effort was appropriately rewarded. The trick is defining what a meaningful reward is and also how we measure effort. Effort may be the animation time it takes to land a heavy attack. In this case, the reward is a larger amount of damage dealt and possibly a knockback or knockdown animation. Effort can be completing a tough, thirty-minute mission with a character three levels lower than the mission recommendation. In this case the player went above and beyond and is expecting an appropriate reward. So, if the game gives them level-restricted weapons they can't use, it sends the message "You shouldn't be here and we don't want you here yet" instead of "You're amazing. Here's your awesome!" There's a lot of risk in sending the former to your players, but the reason developers do this lies with the next two forms of system balance, challenge progression and economy balance.

Challenge progression is focused on maintaining engagement throughout the experience, from each individual encounter to how the challenge progresses across the entire experience. With a lackluster challenge, players can get bored easily. Making the experience too challenging can lead to frustration. The goal for a game designer is to keep the player engaged by giving new mechanics to learn or increasing the complexity of the challenge. The moment both of these plateau is the moment players begin to wonder why they're still playing.

Economy balance has the goal of ensuring players don't earn too much or too little. The economy can be currency, resources, experience points (XP), or really any number-based system in which players can have gains and may have losses. The trick is always to give players enough so they feel satisfied but are always wanting more. Balancing an economy generally requires spreadsheets laying out the designer's expectations for earning and spending, comparing those spreadsheets to the telemetry received from playtests to prove they are on track, and qualitative data to confirm they are hitting the right player experience. Junior designers may not be able to balance complex economies, but they should be able to understand the basics enough to identify individual problems and solve them.

Systems balance comes in many forms and is something designers should always strive for. To do this, they must ensure they have the variables necessary to easily tune any system.

Advanced

What separates good design from great design? In my experience, it's about how much they can build with very little and about how deeply connected everything is in their world. More senior designers need to offer the following skills.

Develop Deep Mechanics. Coming up with new player mechanics is surprisingly easy. And many projects will do it until running out of buttons on the controller. For deep mechanics, the goal is to do a lot with very little. Every new mechanic has a high cost in terms of development and onboarding. Instead of thinking up a new mechanic to solve a problem, senior designers will focus on expanding the old ones. To develop deep mechanics, always ask these questions:

- How can we further challenge our current mechanics?
- What mechanics can be expanded to solve this new problem?
- Are there any mechanics that can be merged and yield the same results?
- How can players use mechanics together to have a deeper experience?
- What modifiers can alter the effect of a mechanic to increase opportunities?

I'll always see Nintendo as the best developer when it comes to designing deep mechanics. In *Super Mario Bros.* (Nintendo, 1985), they were able to create an entire experience out of a simple jump mechanic that covered navigation, attack, dodge, find item, and break environment. The jump mechanic was modified by button press, sprint, and character size, and it allowed for jump combos that could earn extra lives. Not only were the developers able to make a fully engaging experience in *Super Mario Bros.* with that single jump mechanic, but they also took *Super Mario Odyssey* (Nintendo, 2017) to another level by reimagining jump across tons of transformations. The simplest goal when pushing for deep mechanics is: to reduce the number of verbs and increase what they can do.

Develop Deep System Interplay. The developer Ubisoft always pushes for deep system interplay or what they call *systemic systems*. The goal is to develop systems with rules that are so interconnected that emergent experiences occur when multiple systems meet. Some teams call this *sandbox gameplay*.

There are two ways to achieve deep system interplay. One way is to **design systems that have many discrete interactions** with each other. For example, metal attracts lighting, lighting strikes cause sparks, and sparks can catch wood on fire. These discrete rules can lead to exciting scenarios depending on where you plant your metal sword. This approach can be found in games like *The Legend of Zelda: Breath of the Wild* (Nintendo, 2017).

The other method to deep system interplay **utilizes open rules that can offer a lot of overlap**. This approach can be found in games like *Far Cry 3* (Ubisoft, 2012). For example, a lion will attack any non-lion lifeform within twenty meters. This simple rule opens that system to allow for emergent experiences. Let's add more depth and say that the lion will drag any prey under thirty pounds back to its den. Now let's imagine a scenario in which the player sets up a lifelike decoy to draw the attention of nearby military non-player characters (NPCs). After the decoy is set, the player gets into position to ambush the military combatants but then notices their decoy being dragged away by a lion. Although this may be a minor frustration, it also becomes a story the player can share with friends. The experience is even better if that decoy was expensive and so the player chases the lion back to its den.

These types of emergent experiences are the main reason to build deep system interplay. They require the designer to create common attributes for the game's elements (like *lifeform* or *burnable* or *magnetic*) and rules for how these behave and are interacted with. The simplest goal when pushing for deep system interplay is to create a living world. Your systems should feel alive. They should breathe, think, eat, and react. Nature ends up being the best reference as everything in nature interacts in complex ways.

How to Develop Rules, Mechanics, and Systems Skills

Strengthening your ability to design rules, mechanics, and systems requires mental practice. Here are some cheap and effective opportunities to better hone these skills:

Apply Real-World Logic. One of the easiest ways to better understand systems is to look at the world around us. One day in Toronto, I was trying to cross a street when I became frustrated by a walk signal that wouldn't turn on unless I hit the button. The cars going the same direction would get their green light, but the pedestrian sign would still say, "Don't Walk" for me if I forgot to hit the button. A majority of Toronto's lights don't work like this. So why did this one?

The world around us is filled with systems designed by hard-working people. They are the product of centuries of city planning. If they seem frustrating to you then that may mean you aren't the priority they were designed for. In my earlier example, the street I was trying to cross had a high density of traffic. That street was the priority. The street I was walking along had low density. Its light was designed to go green for short moments unless a pedestrian also hit the button. Without the pedestrian hitting the button, the green light wouldn't stay on long enough for pedestrians to safely cross the road. This system was optimized to keep the busy street moving while allowing short windows for cross traffic to go. Next time you come across a system in the real world or a game that leads to frustration, try to identify why the system works the way it does before attempting to redesign it mentally.

Alter Board Games. In Chapter 1 I talked about altering *Monopoly* and all the things that break when making that attempt. Although changing the game was futile in that example, the practice of altering games is an easy way to explore rules, mechanics, and systems. So take out your favorite board game and "break it." Take one of its major rules or mechanics and alter it in a big way. What are the effects for the rest of the experience? Clean up the mess by designing around the break. Keep fixing the issues that arise until you have a very new way to play the game. Then test out your new rendition with friends. When you're ready, build a brand-new board game of your own.

Play Trading Card Games (TCGs). Playing TCGs is one of the best ways to develop your system-building skills and it's one I recommend to all the designers I work with. Building your own deck is equivalent to building a system. You have to operate within numerous limitations and rules, and each card is a mechanic that brings a unique purpose. As you test your deck against others, you'll find flaws and holes, incidents you didn't plan for while building it that need to be remedied if you want to turn that loss into a victory in the future. *Magic: The Gathering* (Wizards of the Coast, 1993) is my usual go-to simply because of the sheer complexity of decks that can be made. Each loss is really a design learning experience. Each win is validation that you're building good systems.

Creative Problem Solving

All designs should be focused on problems that need to be solved. This practice ensures every new design makes the experience work and helps you reach a finished product instead of opening countless other questions. The first step in creative problem solving is identifying the problem and then its cause and finally solving it in a way that creates a better experience without creating new issues. When designers approach design from the perspective of "What problem are we trying to solve?" they create a better experience instead of creating more problems.

Basics

Whenever designers hear an idea, they will almost always jump to the ways it won't work. It's easier to poke holes and tear something apart than it is to build it up. But our job as game designers is to figure out how something *can work.* We must solve problems in order to build something strong and, in my experience, every problem has a solution. Here's what I expect from junior and intermediate game designers in this area.

Don't Trust Your Gut. We all get that gut instinct when something feels off about an idea, the small feeling in the back of our minds that "this won't work" or "I don't like that." Junior designers will let that intuition drive their decisions. Being driven by intuition may work out some of the time but it can also lead to missed opportunities and worse outcomes. Intuition isn't magic. It's your subconscious recognizing patterns based on all of your previous experiences. It spots something it believes you've seen before and screams at your conscious mind. In the real world this intuition helps us survive. But in a creative field where every project has completely different goals, systems, and experiences, it can be wrong a lot.

As junior game designers progress through the field, they must focus on determining what triggered that gut feeling instead of blindly following it. Always ask yourself, "Why won't this work?" or "What don't I like about it?" This takes a lot of practice but over time you'll be able to have deeper conversations about the actual problem rather than stopping with a gut reaction.

Run Mental Scenarios. When most people hear about a design, they'll run the experience over in their mind. It's a skill almost everyone has. A game designer runs those scenarios until all paths are solved, each time throwing a different "What if?" at the situation by setting up a different scenario or making a different decision. For example a designer might ask, "What if the player doesn't see this feedback?" or "What if they're out of ammo?" The more experience we have, the bigger our list of questions gets as we play out scenario after scenario.

Running mental scenarios can be a great way to spot potential problems before going too far down the rabbit hole. The only issue is that, until you actually play the experience, it can be difficult to determine how big or likely these problems actually are. Nothing beats playing the game. So, while running mental scenarios is great practice, don't get too bogged down in these mental gymnastics. When in doubt, prototype it out.

Develop Surgical Solutions. It may be obvious at this point, but a pet peeve of mine is a game designer pitching a "cool" idea. Mostly, this irks me because what they're about to pitch is subjective and almost always causes more problems than it solves. That assessment may seem harsh, but when it comes to game designers, I'm not looking for cool ideas. I'm looking for cool design.

Cool design is that last puzzle piece that fits perfectly and answers all open questions. It solves the problem without causing new ones. It hits all our goals and fits our vision while building toward a better player experience. It's something the team believes in that will get us a major step closer to the finish line. Cool design is extremely difficult to pull off but it starts with hitting each problem head on without the subjective fluff. Once you have a short list of solutions then make sure they're hitting your goals and tackling the vision. Ideas are cheap. Solutions are everything.

Advanced

Senior designers are hungry for tough problems to solve. They are ready and excited to make something work that doesn't initially look like it can or will.

Identify Root Cause. The root cause is the true source of a problem. To find it successfully we need to fight our tendency to speculate about cause and solution at the same time. We've all been in those situations when someone identifies a problem and our response is "We could do this or solve it this way or try this." All our lives we've solved problems. And we've been raised in classrooms to believe that whoever raises their hand first with the solution is the winner. To advance our skills in problem solving and searching out the root cause we need to get past this warped notion and take our time. It's better to be right than to be fast. It's better to measure ten times and prototype once than to measure once and prototype ten times.

To more successfully identify the root cause, we must first gather data on player behavior. Who identified the problem? How was it noticed? How many players are having that problem? Our goal is to collect enough data to recognize and identify patterns. These patterns will lead us to the root cause by pointing out systems that are misunderstood, misaligned, unbalanced, or altogether not being triggered.

Once we've identified a cause, we must understand that this is just our hypothesis. It isn't proven until we've resolved that cause and the problem has actually disappeared. Being more open to this process will ensure you don't get married to solutions or too bogged down in being right. It's more important that the problem be solved successfully.

Stay Ahead of the Problem. Senior game designers solve eighty percent of the problems before the design is written. They do this by identifying the cause and sifting through all possible solutions while keeping in mind the game vision, gameplay vision, and all connections with other features. It takes a lot of practice to keep all of this in your mind while building out a single design. And the truth is, the best designers don't put it all on themselves. They work with the other designers and developers around them, gathering feedback and working things out. The bigger the game is, the more difficult it becomes to manage the entire vision. Becoming more senior doesn't mean you're expected to handle bigger tasks by yourself. You're expected to work smarter, not harder.

Developing Creative Problem-Solving Skills

The only way to become better at problem solving is to get more experience solving problems. And I've found the easiest way of finding problems is to create them yourself.

Improve on Real-World Design. Amazing design is all around us. But instead of looking at the world as designs, look at it as the current solution. While walking around town, spot any element and ask, "Why is that the optimal solution?" or "What would happen if I changed it?" or most importantly "Can I come up with a better option?"

1. Why are manhole covers round? Is that the optimal solution?
2. What would happen if I changed a four-way stop into a roundabout?

3. Fire hydrants take up possible parking spots. Is there a better way?

These questions are meant to spark deeper thoughts on why something is the way it is and help you discover the problems that arise when you try to make changes. Feel free to ponder those three questions before reading the following responses:

1. Manhole covers are round so they won't fall into the hole. If they were square, then the cover could be rotated in a way where it could fall through. Also, dropping a circular manhole cover on the hole will always allow it to settle appropriately. Any other shape and there could be a lot of work readjusting the cover. That being said, is a hole in the street the optimal solution to begin with? It provides easy access but also disturbs traffic whenever work needs to be done.

2. Turning a four-way stop into a roundabout is an interesting opportunity, but let's look at the high-level issues. Standard roundabouts take up more space as they provide medians to separate entry and exit lanes and direct traffic. If you still want a sidewalk, you'll most likely need to take property from the building owners at each corner. You'll also need to ensure the drivers in the area understand how roundabouts work. I'll be honest—as an American/Canadian in his thirties, I have never come across a roundabout while being the driver. This may mean that roundabouts will require more signage than the current four stop signs.

3. Is there a way to design fire hydrants so they don't take up parking spots? The goal of these types of questions isn't necessarily to find the perfect solution but to brainstorm options and identify the problems with each idea. Can we build fire hydrants into stop signs or next to stoplights? Then they'd only be on the corners, which would give buildings less access when needed. What about building them

higher so they could be reached over the average car? That might make it more difficult for firefighters to connect a hose. Maybe this problem can be solved another way or maybe the fire hydrant is the optimal solution. The goal is to keep brainstorming for better solutions without creating new problems.

Troubleshoot. Troubleshooting is a great way to find the root cause of a problem, and it's an easy thing to practice. Searching for the root cause by stepping through a system and checking each connection is logical. If the TV doesn't turn on when you use the remote, the first step is to ensure the remote is correctly pointing at the TV and to press again. Then you'll press harder and for longer just to make sure the problem isn't a button-pressing issue. Some people may give up here as getting up from the couch is just not worth it. But not you! You'll walk over to the TV and press the power button on the device itself. If that works, then something is wrong with the remote. Maybe the batteries need to be replaced. But if the TV didn't turn on, then you'll check to see if the TV is plugged in or if the power cable was chewed through by your beloved pet. If everything looks fine, then that's when you'll probably start freaking out.

This systematic approach is generally the best way to find which piece of a system is the culprit. The only issue is that it requires a lot of knowledge about how the system functions. The less knowledge you have, the sooner you'll hit a dead end. For example, are you prepared to open up the TV to continue tracking the issue?

Your goal as a game designer should be to understand how all of your developed systems function. If you load into your game and a gun doesn't shoot, what's the first thing you would check? How far could you get before you hit a dead end? Troubleshooting is one of the many reasons developers build virtual gyms that offer easy access to test all the aspects of a system. The issue might just be that one gun. The issue might be tuning. The issue might be the ammo system. The issue might be that visual effects (VFX) aren't triggering and the gun is actually working. The entire purpose is to step through these tests quickly and efficiently to find the cause.

To practice, you can easily just look around your house for inspiration. What would happen if you went to the kitchen sink and the water didn't turn on? What would you check? How far could you get before needing to call for help? As a designer, you should develop an inner drive to understand all the systems around you as deeply as possible—especially the ones you use every day.

Prototyping & In-Engine Development

Prototypes and in-engine development are extremely important parts of the design process. Being able to prove out designs and support them without a lot of dev assistance allows you to work quickly and efficiently. Every video game designer must be able to get into the engine and contribute to the development of their features. This doesn't mean you need to be the main programmer. But you will need a solid understanding of tuning and scripting to bring those features to life.

Basics

Junior designers are expected to understand the importance and goals of prototypes. Although they may not be as technically savvy as senior designers, they must still excel at developing prototypes quickly and efficiently. Often this means developing them with any tools they have available.

Prototype with Paper. Many paper prototypes use dice, cards, and paper. Most paper prototypes try to build a card game or board game version of the experience. Although this may feel like the poor man's prototype, there are many examples of paper prototypes being the most effective and efficient option. Iterating on a paper prototype can be as simple as telling the players different rules and using a pencil to alter the board quickly.

I've found that paper prototypes really excel at proving out player motivations when it comes to groups of players needing to work together. Building multiplayer experiences can always be a time-sapping effort when developing a game. Being able to create a simple board-game version of the experience can help designers test the loops, progression, and motivation of the gameplay experience.

Prototype with Apps. The goal of the prototype is to prove out the design's goals and determine if you've solved the problem in the shortest path possible. Designers can use many simple apps to prove out prototypes quickly with mockups and simulations.

Creating mockups is an effective way to get the team to see a solution even if they can't feel it. And with videos mockups we can push the envelope on what people can "feel." Mockups are less useful to prototype gameplay, but they're extremely useful when prototyping user interface. Image and paint software like Adobe Photoshop will allow you to create stills that can showcase heads-up display (HUD) variations. You can take these kinds of mockups even further with more interactive programs like Adobe XD. With XD you can easily prototype simple UI interactions and even puzzles. Video editing software like Adobe After Effects and Blender will allow you to capture in-game footage and create paintovers to showcase how something will actually feel in the game. All of these strategies can help you quickly iterate and prove out a direction before taking the more expensive route of putting it in-game.

Simulations allow you to prototype systems and basic player interactions (mechanics) with those systems. I've seen an entire role-playing game (RPG) progression system simulated via Microsoft Excel Macros, crafting mechanics and flow showcased in Adobe XD, and complex AI simulations developed quickly in web apps. There are many ways to prove out a design before needing to dive into the game engine and build it. In some situations, I prefer to develop prototypes outside the engine. Doing so can allow you to stay focused on the effectiveness of the design and proving the solution. Building in-engine may bring the trap of proving out implementation rather than design.

Tune. Tuning is about altering the variables of a feature until it works as intended. Tuning may be used to correct the damage of a weapon, the number of enemies in an encounter, or the animation speed of an attack.

I've seen a simple tuning change turn a hated feature into an exciting addition to the game. Having a solid vision comes into play again: Knowing how the experience should feel and how it should be balanced against all other systems is key to ensuring its success. If something isn't working, don't be discouraged. That's when your skills really need to kick in. Also, if something *is* working, don't be complacent. Try to take the feature even further until you break it. Only by testing the boundaries of a feature can you truly understand the tuning sweet spot. I've seen too many designers increase a number and stop once they were satisfied. But what would have happened if they had kept going? How do they know it wouldn't get even better? Good designers know the lower and upper limits of their features.

Don't let features go into the dev build without taking a first pass at tuning. First impressions are important. I've seen designers focus on designs and prototypes outside the build while letting the dev build itself fall apart. Every developer is playing in the dev build, and the longer they see and feel subpar features, the more they'll wonder if the game design is on the right track. Your highest priority is keeping the dev build playable and aligned with the vision.

Advanced

Both intermediate and senior designers should utilize this section. Designers won't get very far in this industry without being able to develop in the engine.

Apply in-Engine Prototyping & Scripting. Being able to develop in the engine is an important and required skill. Major developers will generally have their own in-house engines, which can be a bonus or a boon. In-house engines are developed over multiple projects and specifically for a developer's games. So utilizing their engine to work on their specific titles should be a breeze—should be. These engines and their tools will almost always come with a lot of baggage from previous titles and teams that have used them. The trick to developing in these engines is to determine what you can and can't touch. Ask the engineers for this information and also find out the best way to prototype and script inside the engine. In my experience, many of these engines can be houses of cards, and you don't want to be the one who blows them over.

Intermediate and senior game designers should be able to, and are expected to, build prototypes to prove concepts within their specialization. Gameplay designers should be able to prototype their mechanics, AI designers should be able to script AI, and so on. Again, the intention for prototypes is to prove that the design successfully solved the problem and fits the goals. The intention isn't to determine how the feature should be implemented. Separating those two intentions can help you save a lot of time.

Learn Coding. It will always be in the best interest of game designers to gain a basic understanding of C# and C++. Many free sources online can teach you how to code, and free versions of Visual Studio can help with most basic needs.

Understanding the basics of programming will help you have better conversations with the programmers on your team. I'm not saying you'll be able to keep up when the conversations turn to threads, memory leaks, or running time. But you will be better able to understand the complexity of your requests and, at times, help pitch ways of reusing or repurposing work.

How to Develop Prototyping and in-Engine Skills

It's never been easier to gain the technical skills necessary to succeed in this industry. You can find resources in online videos, free software, games, and even free engines. All you need is the willingness to learn in a challenging and technical environment.

Turn Video Games into Paper Games. To increase your skills with paper prototypes, take your favorite video game moments and turn them into board games, card games, or even dice games. I don't mean that you should turn the entire video game into a board game (unless you really want to go through that effort). But simply take one moment in the game to prototype. As an example, I'll turn to one of my personal favorites: The Battle of Narshe party split system in *Final Fantasy VI* (Square, 1994):

What is the experience?

- A group of enemies is trying to get past you to kill a VIP. Multiple routes exist for the enemies to reach the VIP. Split your group of warriors into multiple parties to stop the enemy advance. Don't let a single one get past you.

What are we proving via the prototype (design goals)?

- Ensuring players appreciate the capabilities and benefits of each warrior they control (archetypes) and don't focus solely on a single party of their favorites.
- Adding a compelling layer of strategy on top of the standard combat system
    - Party split strategy
    - Party movement strategy

What is the setup?

- **Goal:** The player must keep enemies from reaching the VIP. An enemy leader will remain at the base of the mountain. Kill the leader to win.
- **Board Setup:** Large boulders split the mountainside into many different paths up to the VIP position. Do we need a visual grid to track movement?
- **Enemy Setup:** Twelve groups of enemies will make their way up the mountain. The setup offers different types of enemy groups: common, elite, leader. How can we distinguish them?
- **Warrior Setup:** Seven player-controlled warriors of varying archetypes exist: two mages, three soldiers, two rogues. How do they differ in abilities?
- **Player Setup:** Players choose how to split their warriors into three parties. Seven warriors exist, each with their own stats and skills. A party can hold a max of four warriors. How can the player keep track of who is in what party?

What is the play?

- **Game Loop**: Position > Battle > Advance
- **Position**: The player will take a turn moving each of their parties and then move the enemies based on designed rules. The VIP and enemy leader don't move. How many squares can the player's team move? How many for enemies? What's the design for enemy movement?
- **Battle**: Combat is not what we are trying to prove with this prototype so it shouldn't be a heavy focus. What's the easiest way to determine a winner quickly when two opposing groups meet that also takes into account the different warrior archetypes within a group?
- **Advance**: Do any health systems persist outside of combat? Is there an eminent loss state that players can't come back from? How can we easily increase and decrease the challenge?

What is the finish?

- **Win**: The player defeats the enemy leader in combat.
- **Loss**: An enemy reaches the VIP.

The purpose of this exercise is to gain experience turning video game mechanics and systems into paper versions for quick prototyping. But don't forget that there are opportunities other than board games. Can you turn the basic attacks and defense of *Street Fighter* (Capcom, 1987) into a gesture-based game à la RPS? Can you turn a boss encounter from *Demon's Souls* (FromSoftware, 2009) into a card and dice game? With enough practice you'll be able to prototype your experiences quickly and better solidify your gameplay loops before needing to commit to more costly forms of development.

Explore Modding Tools. My first foray into modding tools was with *Neverwinter Nights* (BioWare, 2002). I remember opening its Aurora Toolset and being blown away as well as completely lost. With those tools I explored narrative, scripting, level design, and AI setups. My first goal was to remake the labyrinth from one of my favorite games, *King's Quest VI* (Sierra Entertainment, 1992). But instead of the labyrinth ending with a minotaur, I would end it with dragons. I slowly explored the toolset and was able to build an experience and share it with the online player base. The dungeon master feature allowed me to watch others play what I built, so I also consider this my first observed playtest. Sadly, that's when I learned that the game had an in-depth character modding system that allowed online players to create invincible characters. My first foray into creating a gameplay experience was torn through in seconds.

Modding tools are an amazing resource for gamers who want to make the transition into developers. Your first try will be overwhelming and your first creation will most likely stink. But the knowledge gained and accomplishments achieved will be well worth it.

Learn Unity & Unreal. Unity and Unreal Engine are two very accessible engines for anyone looking to dive deeper into game development. They offer great tools and easy jumping-off points for getting a prototype up and running quickly. Many designers I know find it easier to prove out designs in these engines rather than the in-house engines their games are being developed in.

In my opinion, the biggest draw for these engines isn't their ease of use but the ease of access to training and documentation. YouTube offers tons of tutorials posted from developers all over the world. At this point, there's no reason not to learn at least one of these engines. That knowledge can only help you as you develop your skills as a game designer.

Learn Logic Design. In college I took an electrical engineering course that revolved around logic design. Logic design is the basis of all circuitry, computer systems, and computer algorithms. It also becomes the basis of all systems design when designing games. Although AND, OR, XOR, and NOT gates are all pretty simple concepts, entire industries and fields of study use them as their base. Not only should this be a subject you dive further into, but it should also be an inspiration that these four "mechanics" can create so many experiences.

If you want to stay away from classrooms and engineering (you shouldn't), then you can always look to redstone blocks in *Minecraft*. Redstone blocks offer the "electrical signals" you need to explore the world of circuitry and logic design.

Analyzing the Market

As game designers, we must always look at our industry with a professional eye. The role of game designer requires a deep understanding of who your specific market is. Knowing your market, the games within it, and which games are dominating and why are requirements to building a successful experience for that market. Without this knowledge, you're likely to build an experience for *yourself*. Although building an experience for yourself *can* lead to success, it's more likely to lead to headaches as you test it with actual consumers.

Basics

I've seen many designers have difficulty going beyond a hobbyist mentality in order to become the professional game designer they need to be. Play everything, reference anything. At the most basic level you are expected to play and analyze the top games in your genre and the top games in the industry overall.

Use Deep Analysis. Analyzing a game has nothing to do with what you liked or disliked about the experience. Analyzing ends when you have a deep understanding of what makes that game tick. This includes all the mechanics, systems, and rules that make up the experience as well as the gameplay loops that drive it. The goal is to understand better why that dev team made the decisions they made and, more importantly, what their market enjoys about that experience. By doing this we are building a library of knowledge that we can pull from later on for our own designs.

Identify Trends. As designers we must always understand what is currently trending in today's market—not only what it is, but also where it came from and why it is successful. With this knowledge, we'll be able to utilize and build off of popular features, systems, and mechanics that are being enjoyed by the industry today. It also allows us to discuss best practices and what may be popular in the future.

For example, what is battle royale? What title/mod started the concept? What industry trends came beforehand that paved the way for it? Why is it successful? What is it offering that didn't exist before? Who was playing it before it was successful? The answers to these questions may help you identify trends earlier and get ahead of trends in the future. Professional game designers should always be studying the industry and searching for these answers.

Advanced
Game designers must strive to develop games as a profession as well as a hobby. Your passion needs to revolve around making games that people love to play, not making games only for yourself. Senior designers immerse themselves in their market.

Design for Personas/Cohorts. Player personas and cohorts are ways of grouping players who enjoy similar types of games or have comparable gaming habits. They allow you to better identify your market by categorizing them. Most games cater to multiple personas at once. Keeping groups of players happy who are motivated by different things is a constant challenge. For example, some gamers play *Destiny* (Bungie Inc, 2014) for the linear player vs. environment (PvE) experience and stop there. Others grind loot and try to outfit themselves with the best gear. Another group may solely focus on the player vs. player (PvP) modes. Designing for each of these groups is a challenge, especially when you want each of them to dip into the other areas of the game.

Personas allow you to understand player behaviors and specify who your new feature is for. Looking through your feature list may reveal that most features lean toward a couple of personas, leaving the others with little to enjoy. This imbalance may be a problem you need to rectify. Understanding the specific market and consumer personas for your project is a powerful tool. It will allow you to design with specific players in mind instead of a generic idea.

Innovate on Trends. Many developers try to follow trends, but few ever innovate on them. Following a trend means developing a game that incorporates the same formula as a modern, successful title while also adding a key differentiator. That differentiator could be a different fantasy, progression system, or major mechanic. If developers are fast enough, they may be able to capitalize on an existing trend. But are they innovating on it?

Innovation requires a deeper understanding of why the experience is trending in the first place. For instance, battle royale is a highly competitive PvP experience in which every minute of survival feels like a victory. It is filled with players achieving new personal goals:

- I've never survived this long before.
- I've never killed another player before.
- I've never been this highly ranked.
- I won! (the gameshow moment)

But what makes battle royale shine is the fact that it pushes the player between constant extreme emotions like tension and excitement in a deadly, PvP environment, making it fun to stream and play. By understanding the core aspects that lead to battle royale's success, a game designer can separate those key pieces from the game mode itself. Then, by reimagining these pieces, the game designer can innovate upon the trend. Such innovation is seen in games like *Escape from Tarkov* (Battlestate Games, 2017).

How to Develop Market Analysis Skills

Increasing your knowledge of the market seems like an easy thing to do. But examining the market's games without understanding gameplay loops, mechanics, systems, and vision, may mean that you're simply playing games instead of analyzing them.

Play Everything, Reference Anything. Every game you play expands your library of gaming knowledge. Every new game you pick up should be seen as an opportunity to learn. That doesn't mean the experience can't also be fun. It does mean we shouldn't stick to the same games and genres on repeat. We are students of the industry. And to embrace this industry we need to go outside of our comfort zones and explore:

- **Mods** built by the community are where we see the biggest innovations due to their fast iteration and instant response from the market. *League of Legends* (Riot Games, 2009) sprang from *Defense of the Ancients (Steve Freak & Icefrog, 2003)*, which started as a mod of *Warcraft III: Reign of Chaos (Blizzard Entertainment, 2002)*. PlayerUnknown's Battlegrounds (PUBG Corporation, 2017) was first a mod of *DayZ* (Bohemia Interactive, 2013), which in turn started as a mod of *ARMA 2* (Bohemia Interactive, 2009). At this point, any new idea you can think up is probably a mod in *Minecraft*.

- **Indie games** will always show thinking outside the box and they are a great place to reference depth in mechanics. These developers are thrifty and don't let an ounce of their mechanics go to waste as can be seen in games like *Braid* (Jonathan Blow, 2008) and *FTL: Faster than Light* (Subset Games, 2012). Games like *Papers, Please* (Lucas Pope, 2013) will always make you wonder, "Who would ever make a game about this and why do I love it so much?"

- **Mobile games** are where we'll spot the best retention and monetization mechanics the industry has to offer. They are also the fastest changing market, so what's successful today may be gone in a week.

- **Casino slots** could be considered the best games at monetization. I use the term "best" loosely. And some may question whether they are even games. But I've recently seen cooperative slots in which all connected machines are building spaceships to defend Earth from the next alien invasion in three minutes. Some slot machines print out tickets as save files to maintain your progression in a storyline. Casinos are pulling from the video game industry more and more.

- **AAA releases** will always push the envelope on graphics, scope, blockbuster narratives, and the feel of flawless 3Cs (character, camera, controls). They are also one of the slowest-changing sectors as big publishers rely more on sequels and following trends than on advancing the industry.

Each of these media will be around for a long time. If you really want to design best-in-class experiences, broaden your horizons and understand every corner of this great industry. For game designers, spending one hundred plus hours on the same game should not be seen as a badge of honor; instead, it represents missed opportunities.

Follow Key Sites, Forums, & Streamers. To understand the market, we must immerse ourselves in it. Gaming news sites and forums allow us to be up to date on top industry news and get a pulse on what's trending. I'm not referring to cosplay forums, although I'm sure some will argue there's validity in knowing what's trending there as well.

Another great avenue is Gamespot's *Trax Newsletter,* which is a monthly report on the top-trending games based on awareness and purchase intent. It's a good way to see what's popular in the AAA space.

Watching streamers and content creators is a newer way to consume game content. Like many developers my age, the first time I heard about streamers I was confused. Why would you watch other people play games instead of playing them yourself? Then I remembered my love for *Mystery Science Theater 3000* and my time spent watching reaction videos to Childish Gambino's "This Is America." Watching someone play a video game offers two forms of entertainment and an opportunity to learn from top players.

The hard skills listed in this chapter are what I try to ingrain in every designer I mentor. In my experience, the designers who excel at these skills are better equipped to take on the job and progress through their careers. But without the soft skills to compliment these hard skills, many designers are still held back from achieving their full potential.

CHAPTER 15

CORE SOFT SKILLS

Soft skills are generally synonymous with communication skills. But game designers must go beyond simply communicating their vision. The days of dictating the design and using your position to push your will are over. I'm honestly not sure they ever existed. As game designers, we need to inspire and lead above all else or the team will lose passion, and the game will suffer.

After seeing where most dev teams fail in the development process, I consider soft skills to be just as important as hard skills. This chapter will discuss each core soft skill, the competencies expected of junior to senior designers, and ways to develop each skill further. We'll consider three key soft skills:

- Driving the gameplay experience
- Collaborative design
- Pitching & selling

Driving the Gameplay Experience

Game designers drive the gameplay experience from start to finish. The process starts as a vision, is designed into a game, and through countless iterations is developed into a shippable experience. The further you push a team through that process, the more ownership you must give to the team. And the more features you drive, the more leadership skills are required to see success.

Basics

Junior and intermediate designers will focus on driving the gameplay experience of individual features. Succeeding at the following abilities will showcase your skill in this area and determine whether you're ready for a bigger mandate.

Champion the Vision. Championing a vision involves two subskills: communicating and policing. To ensure successful communication, you must develop a clear and concise vision that every team member can easily understand. The easiest way to test a vision's clarity is to pitch it to someone and ask them to explain it back to you.

At times, large teams operate like a giant game of telephone. The only way to get to the finish line with an intact message is to keep that message simple. When testing and building your vision, make sure you change up who you're pitching it to in order to receive varied feedback. Always search out new people who think differently than you. If you find someone who doesn't agree with the vision, that's a great thing. This is the type of person you want to go to more regularly. They think differently than you and will offer more unique insights.

To police the vision, you'll need to stay up to date on the status of all your features and related features. This way you can be sure the features are coming together as expected. Also, by staying apprised of what's making it into the build, you'll be in a better position to spot decisions that don't align with the vision. When this happens, you'll want to have a conversation with the developer about the vision, not just about the decision that went awry. The misalignment occurred because the developer doesn't understand the vision or doesn't believe in it. This is the actual problem to solve. If it isn't solved, then these types of issues will continue to occur. Solving this problem may require you to update your vision to ensure clarity. If everyone understands and believes in the vision, then they'll be more likely to make decisions that align. Conversely, if you're unhappy with a developer's decision even though it technically aligns with the vision, then your vision is faulty.

Build Useful Documentation. Designers will always hit a point during development when they need to switch from early conception prototypes to formalized design documentation. Two realizations always trigger this switch:

- The vision and design become too complex to maintain via memory alone.
- Tribal knowledge doesn't scale.

Design teams that don't make the switch at the right moment will always feel the pain, either by forgetting areas that were already designed or by seeing things get messy across the team. On the other hand, using design docs too early may slow down the open prototype phase that every conception needs. You can generally find the sweet spot by listening to the team. When questions about the design start ramping up, it's time for documentation.

I've worked at many studios, and each studio has had its own format for documentation. But almost every studio has the same issue where a majority of the developers don't care to read that documentation. My favorite format leans into this problem by making the first document of every feature a presentation. This presentation is generally a ten-slide deck that gives an overview of the gameplay experience provided by the feature. The deck is meant to be presented, not read. The presentation gives another opportunity to inspire the team with the goals and purpose of the design. You can also share a video of the presentation for anyone who missed it.

No matter the format of documentation, game designers need to build and upkeep it to maintain knowledge of the current designs and intentions. They also must manage its location to ensure the team always has easy access.

Champion Iteration. To champion iteration you need to embrace it. All feedback is valid and all features are open for discussion. Closing doors on either of these can hurt the product in the long run. But it can be frustrating when you're on the twentieth iteration of a feature, everything finally seems to work, and a colleague approaches to request changes. As a designer you need to be as open to that twenty-first iteration request as you were to the first one. That doesn't mean you have to implement it. But you must be open to the conversation and ready to make changes while maintaining all the successes you've built up to that point.

No design is final until the game ships and sometimes not even then. You must be open to all feedback from the team, the publisher, and players. Beyond that openness, you need the skills to process the feedback and understand the intent behind it. Only then can you successfully integrate the feedback into your design.

Advanced

Senior designers will drive larger sections of the game, and directors will drive the gameplay experience as a whole. Leading features and specialties at this scale means taking a larger ownership of the final product. It also requires you to be comfortable with empowering and trusting the team with more ownership as well.

Take Ownership of Problems. As designers, we must take ownership of the entire gameplay experience by ensuring it is successfully coming together and embodying the vision. When senior designers spot a problem in any aspect of the experience, it's their responsibility to say something. They must own that problem until they track down its true owner. If there is none, then they become the owner until they find someone better suited. These problems include any that may exist with goals and features owned by other designers or superiors. Senior designers must successfully manage up to ensure the success of the entire gameplay experience.

Too often we see the "not my problem" approach or "I'm sure somebody's on it." This apathy leads to issues staying unresolved until they cause giant fires or end up shipping in the final product. In order to be in a position to spot these issues and own the gameplay experience, you must look at the entire experience holistically and play the game as often as possible.

Empower the Team. All designers must own the *vision* for their sections and empower the team to own the *game.* It can be difficult releasing control of our features, but we must also trust the expertise of the people around us to take the design to the next level. The best game designers are ones who lean into this form of empowerment but always maintain control of the *vision.*

On many occasions developers will come to you with alternate pitches to the design. This is a great thing as it shows they are still passionate about the end product. When those pitches stop coming is when you need to worry. If you're not receiving feedback, it's not because the design is perfect; it's because nobody cares anymore. Our goal is to keep the team invested and inspired. If you can't convince the tasked programmer about the merits of the approved design, then this is where you must stay until they believe in it or you believe in them. Don't pull the "I'm the designer" card unless you're prepared to have your feature implemented in the worst way possible, with the absolute minimal effort.

If someone has a pitch that they believe fits better, then hear them out. If their pitch still fits your goals, then honestly consider trying it first even if it might cause some minor issues. This is how you build trust. You can't get trust without giving it. The truth is that if the programmer's pitch fails, they'll work that much harder to fix it or switch back to your pitch. Most of the time, this process leads to success with their design or to success from working together to resolve the new issues that may have come up.

Owning the vision and goals allows you to direct the feature and not dictate the design. When you bring a design to the table, be prepared to pitch it, defend it, and pivot as needed.

How to Develop the Skill of Driving an Experience

Driving an experience is a challenging mission. As a team grows, that challenge increases exponentially. To succeed, you need to keep an open dialogue with the team. Once that stops, everything stops.

Learn to Lead. Leadership is one of the most powerful traits you can gain in your life. It's also one you'll never fully master. Every day is a new learning opportunity in which you are reminded to put the team before yourself. Shutting out other developers is not an option. Dictating a design is not an option. Leadership is about raising up the voices of the people around you. It's not about speaking for them or over them. Leadership isn't about having all the answers. Instead, it's about having the humility to say when you don't. And it's about building enough trust with the team that you can lift each other up in those moments.

Every game designer must lead. They don't always lead people, but they do lead the gameplay experience. That means owning the vision for where you're headed as a team. If you make game design all about you, then you'll take heat from all angles when the design fails (and it will fail). If you make game design about the team, then the team will be there when everything falls apart. This is a creative field in which everyone desires to push innovation so things will fail and everything will fall apart.

Start training in leadership today and never stop. I started my training in college with student organizations and I haven't stopped learning since. You can take courses, enroll in programs, go on retreats. But the only way to really learn is to do. Take every leadership opportunity you can. Fail and get back up. But above all else, put the team first.

Test out Different Documentation. Design docs are an essential communication tool. If nobody is reading the design document then it's failing at its job. As designers we are meant to prototype features, see how our player base reacts, and adjust as needed. But when it comes to managing the dev team, we somehow forget this process entirely. Treat the dev environment the same way you treat the game. If nobody wants to read your docs, then consider the documentation a failing feature.

Treat it as another problem that needs to be solved.

To build successful documentation you have to successfully depict the design in a way that all coworkers can understand and you need to prepare the documentation in a medium they'll more readily take in. The medium could be pitch briefs, presentation videos, comic panels, mockups, wireframes, interactive models, or any other format that best gets the design across. If your team isn't interested in your current format, then test out another. Ask for feedback and alter your format until they're in. Finding an optimal way to communicate through documentation will help information spread through your team and reduce the need for redundant meetings.

Collaborative Design

A major part of collaboration is simply frontloading the conversation. Although parts of this book may seem like I'm adding a lot of extra overhead to the design process, I'm really just putting a required conversation where it should be. That conversation will happen no matter what, whether it's at the beginning (best option), in the middle of development, or when the feature is completed and other developers are realizing that it runs counter to what they were working on. It's always best to have the conversation earlier rather than later.

Basics

I expect a lot of collaboration from all game designers on my team, but I always want to make sure the value of collaboration is instilled in junior and intermediate designers early. Game designers shouldn't build designs in a vacuum only to reveal them when completed. Instead, they should acquire feedback and work with seasoned developers to strengthen the design before pitching it to the team.

Accept All Feedback. I've heard designers complain when they ask the dev team for feedback and end up receiving pitches for different designs instead of the "feedback" they requested. They see such feedback as an attack on their role as a game designer. What those designers aren't realizing is that everything is valid feedback. When someone plays your experience and pitches you a design, they are saying that something is missing. Since they aren't a designer, they're not always able to translate their gut feelings into the problem. So they go straight to a solution. In these cases, the easiest response is "What's the problem you're trying to solve?" This sets the conversation down a better path. It's our job as designers to be open to all types of feedback. And most of the time that feedback needs to be talked out and translated.

When we receive feedback, we all have a tendency to defend the current design. And the stronger your goals and design, the easier it is to defend. But it's important to be open to criticism in order to reach the best possible experience. If you find yourself defending a design multiple times from the comments of multiple devs then it's time to take a step back and re-evaluate. For me, I go with the magic number of three.

With the first two devs, I listen to concerns, try to understand their goals, compare them to mine, and discuss how to move forward. The third time I'm questioned about a design decision, I take a hard step back, stop thinking of my goals, and reflect on all those points of feedback from a different perspective. Sometimes this leads to a redesign, sometimes it results in a few additions to shore up concerns, and sometimes we triple down and become more confident in the current approach. But the important part is to know when to take a serious moment of reflection and throw away your preconceived notions.

Search out Ideas & Feedback. It's our job as designers to own the gameplay vision and strive for the best design. It's not our job to have all the ideas or even the best ideas. Ideas are everywhere, and it is our job simply to find them.

For example, let's say you're making a first-person shooter and you're in charge of finalizing a list of forty weapon mods. It's not probable that you, by yourself, are going to come up with the best forty mods that will hugely enhance the gameplay experience. With thousands or even millions of mod ideas possible, you'll probably come up with fewer than one hundred (probably less than forty).

The only hope to coming up with a truly stunning set of mods is to maximize the number of ideas and feedback. This means turning to the team. But you own the vision! So what type of experience are you looking for? What are your goals? How should this all come together? Do you want ten mods for each playstyle or player type you support? Do you want each mod to have a meaningful and noticeable impact on the gameplay experience? Do you want a couple of joke mods or end-game mods that are superpowerful? Hash out all your goals, and when you're ready, share them with the team. Chat with all the related devs one-on-one, talk to different disciplines, and even hold a brainstorm. Brainstorms via forums or emails are ideal for generating low-level idea lists for designs like mods. Send out a call for ideas along with your goals and wait for the ideas to roll in.

For some reason, every new designer feels they need to impress the team with their own amazing ideas. They feel like, if they aren't the one pitching ideas, then they're failing. But the only failure is a poor gameplay experience. It doesn't matter where the ideas come from, just that you brought them together into the rules, mechanics, and systems that made for a great experience. Honestly, it's even better when the ideas come from the team so they feel ownership in the experience too. That being said, give appropriate credit to whoever did come up with the ideas. If you can't remember who, then just say, "Team Effort."

I push my designers to say "Team Effort" even if they did come up with the ideas because it's easy to accidentally think you did even if you didn't. Besides, no one wants to hear a designer pitching the final design while boasting, "I came up with this."

Advanced

The more designers collaborate, the more trust they'll build with the team. That trust is needed to get through the tough times in development when nothing seems to work and nothing is coming together. That's when solid teams collaborate to solve the necessary problems and make something great. That is also when teams without trust fall apart due to infighting. The next skills are what senior designers rely on to unite teams.

Listen First, Talk Last. As we grow in seniority on the design team, our word carries a lot more weight. This can be an advantage when driving meetings and leading features, but it can also shut down a conversation and cause us to miss out on great input. In meetings where everyone is sharing feedback and pitching ideas, try to always be the last to talk. Listen to everyone's thoughts and incorporate them into your final thoughts. There's great power in everyone knowing they're being heard and even more power in building the expectation that you'll have the final thoughts and decision in the end.

Although I have witnessed the power of this skill firsthand, it's also a lesson I have to relearn in almost every meeting with other directors. Riffing back and forth with a group of your peers is fun and exciting, but at times I find myself stomping others in the conversation. The key is to realize when you're doing it and then to make a conscious effort to take a back seat and listen. It's also helpful to call on the names of silent individuals to ensure their input is being heard.

Never Compromise the Vision. As designers we should be open to all feedback and ideas, but that doesn't mean we should accept changes that go against the vision. Doing this will usually lead to a snowball effect as the changes clash with all other systems still following the vision. Remember: As a game designer, your number-one goal is getting the team to understand and believe in the vision. If you start crossing that vision, then the team will stop believing in you.

Senior designers must always explain when ideas clash with the vision and use it as an opportunity to reinforce confidence in the vision. If a developer pitches you something that goes against the vision, explain the clash. For example:

> "We can't go to a full-screen puzzle in *Dead Space* because we never want to cut away from Isaac's camera. Doing this risks breaking the immersion we've built and can lead to a break in the fourth wall. We'll need to build the puzzle into the world or into a hologram."

Designers should never compromise the current vision unless they're changing it. And if that happens, that change requires tact when communicating it to the team. Up to this point, everyone has been basing their decisions on this vision. Make sure to discuss the change one-on-one with the developers who are impacted the most. If it's a major change that spans across multiple disciplines, be sure to confer with the directors of each discipline and have them discuss it with their devs. When big changes like this aren't communicated well, everything starts to fall apart, including trust.

How to Develop Collaborative Design Skills

The secret to collaboration is to go in knowing you'll end up with something better than what you started with, whether that means iterating on your current design or finding something completely new. The best way to improve this skill is to start listening.

Approach a New Dev Each Day. As designers, we need to collect as many ideas as possible every day. But I've found that interacting with the same people on repeat will lead to the same type of ideas. These echo chambers can make you feel like you're on the right track but end up giving you tunnel vision. Try to always approach someone new to riff on designs even if you don't expect to get anything worthwhile (maybe especially so).

Throughout my career I've come across a few developers who think completely outside the box. Sometimes I even get the feeling they are messing with me. The usual designer response is to shun off wacky ideas and laugh them off. But this is a mistake. You have found someone who thinks completely differently from you. Embrace the difference! These people's different perspective will lead you down avenues you would never come close to otherwise. Most of the time what they say may sound crazy, but there are times when crazy is exactly what you need.

Get away from the echo chambers and start making everyone feel like they're part of the team.

Repeat Everyone's Stance. Whenever someone pitches an idea or solution, try repeating it back to them. Don't just say their words but instead translate them into what they're hoping to achieve. What are the goals they're trying to accomplish?

What's the problem they identified? If you're able to reexplain what they said but in terms of high-level goals, you'll prove that you listened, understood them, and care about their input. This is what earns you respect and trust. Practice this behavior whenever someone pitches you an idea or describes a problem with the experience.

Design Pitching/Selling

As game designers, we must understand the importance of *selling* a design instead of simply communicating it because getting a team to believe in a design is more important than them just understanding it. Belief inspires passion. Passion leads to great games.

Basics
Selling a design can be done with a prototype or a pitch. In the best of times, you may have both. In the worst of times, you'll only have your words. But great game designers can get someone to picture an experience and be excited about a design just by talking it through.

Build Belief. As in any creative field, our designs are completely subjective. What makes your design better than the countless others? This question will come up a lot since every passionate developer will have their own ideas. But belief is a surprisingly easy thing to attain as long as you're using solution-oriented, goal-driven design. To build belief in a design, you'll want to follow these steps when pitching it:

1. **Identify the Problem:** The first step to building belief is to prove that a problem exists. Why add the feature? What issue are you trying to resolve? Even the response, "to add fun" is inherently stating that the game isn't fun enough yet,

which is the identifiable problem. So what is causing the game to not be fun? Is it too slow paced? Not challenging enough? Are the mechanics not engaging? Is the goal not compelling? These would be the specific problems you need to solve. And the more you can identify the root cause, the better. Do not move past this step until everyone believes there is a problem and you've identified it.

2. **Prove It Needs a Solution:** You've identified a problem, but does it need to be solved? Don't assume that it does. Every game will ship with problems. Most of those problems weren't big enough to require solutions. They only caused minor frustrations or were barely noticed. It's only a real problem if everyone agrees that it is. If they don't, then don't worry about the next step until you can convince them that the problem is big enough to need a solution.

3. **Build Your Design Goals:** Once the team is convinced the problem needs a solution, you'll want to build out your other design goals. What else should the design include in order to ensure its success? These should be intentions that everyone can agree will help narrow what is considered an optimal solution. The design goals could be to better sell the player fantasy, to ensure another specific problem doesn't arise, and to drive players into other systems A and B. Just like with the core problem, you should convince everyone of these goals before moving on.

4. **Pitch the Optimal Solution:** Now you must work with the team to design a solution and prove that it's the optimal path forward. *Optimal* means something different to every developer. An artist may think the current design requires too many assets to be considered optimal. An engineer may think it opens too many unknowns. A producer may think it's too risky at this point in the project. To a game designer, *optimal* means it solves the problem without

creating new issues, achieves the design goals, and brings the experience closer to the vision. Optimizing the design is a full team effort, and once the team agrees on an optimal solution, they will work hard to achieve it.

If you follow those steps, then building belief in a design should be simple. Just make sure you hit those beats in the exact order when presenting it:

1. Here is the problem. It looks to be caused by X.
2. It needs to be solved because of Y.
3. We can be successful if we also consider Goals 1, 2, 3.
4. Finally, here's the optimal design that solves the problem and achieves our goals.

At any point in this pitch, people could disagree with your assessment. That's why it's always best to build this pitch alongside other people and iterate on it based on feedback. You'll need these allies when building belief in this creative, subjective environment.

Tell the Story. As you pitch a design, most developers will follow along by imagining the player experience. They will picture the player encountering the feature from start to finish. As designers, we should lean into this approach to ensure everyone is picturing the same thing. If you're pitching a crafting system, don't start by showcasing a list of items the player can craft. Instead, start with how the player gets into the system. If a crafting bench is the entry point into the experience, then that's where the pitch starts.

Step through the experience as if you're the player seeing it for the first time. Tell the story of the player experience. If developers are interrupting your pitch with questions, then you are most likely jumping around too much in the mental story. Having a good story flow should raise questions in the audience's mind that are quickly answered by your next point. The better you get at this skill, the more you'll realize that you can build and completely control the image in everyone's mind. Conveying the player experience is a powerful tool when pitching your designs.

Imagery is also extremely important to ensure everyone is picturing the same experience. When adding images into your pitches or design docs, they should solely focus on ensuring everyone is imagining the same experience.

I've found that telling the story of the creation of the design to be just as powerful as the story of the player experience. For everyone to understand how you came to this exact solution, they sometimes need to understand what you tried before and what led to your current goals. Discussing your previous attempts and failures can be as important as the current success.

Advanced

Senior designers should be able to gain belief from the team without raising major issues. Furthering their skills requires them to focus more on inspiration and clarity.

Inspire. Building belief is a powerful tool and a major step toward inspiring a team. But to truly inspire the entire team you'll want to develop design goals that excite each discipline and entice devs to apply their craft toward those goals. The difficulty is that everyone on the team has different priorities.

To inspire the team, you'll need to build a single pitch for all audiences. Some developers will care about deep systems while others will care about the emotions the player will experience. Some can be excited by a prototype while others may find it difficult to visualize beyond gray boxes and placeholder animation. You must know and pitch to every priority in the room at the same time. This is a difficult skill. Achieving inspiration requires the right pitch, the right presenter, and preferably a strong relationship with the audience.

If you're presenting to a new audience, I've found it best to cover all bases by ensuring your features have goals that hit each of the following categories:

- Fantasy/emotion
- Fun/feel
- Challenge/systems
- Player goals/gameplay loops

Once you better understand your audience, you can optimize your pitches and flow in order to inspire with ease.

Leave No Room for Misinterpretation. Designers tend to consider a pitch successful when everyone is on board. I consider a pitch successful when everyone is picturing the same experience. Too often I've seen a thumbs up from everyone in the room but later realize that each person was picturing something different. This is a failed pitch that will create devastating damage during development as everyone spreads misguided information about the design intentions. It's better to receive a No on a design rather than a misinformed Yes.

Game designers must leave no room for misinterpretation of their pitch. Visuals and simulations are key to ensuring everyone is thinking of the same experience. Use basic imagery and animations or more successful mockups, flowcharts, wireframes, videos, prototypes, or interactive models. As you get to know your audience, you'll better understand which medium works best for them. I highly recommend getting feedback in one-on-one settings, where you can simply ask the developer to explain the experience back to you. This can lead to great insights on the pitch's success.

How to Develop Pitching/Selling Skills

The only way to develop your pitching/selling skills is to build and give pitches.

Build Presentations. Pitch presentations incorporate visual aids and help control pacing and flow. The go-to program for building presentations is PowerPoint, but I've seen designers work wonders with programs like Adobe XD, which was developed for mocking-up apps but offers deeper interactions and transitions. Pick the program you feel can best help you express your designs and dive in. But always make sure that any flair you add to the presentation is there because you need it. Images, animations, and transitions should be there to help you showcase design intent not to wow the audience with random light shows.

In the future, instead of using standard text-based design docs, try building a five- to ten-minute presentation to sell the player experience. When done right, it can build a stronger image in everyone's minds better than a Word doc.

Pitch to an Empty Room. I've found the only way to memorize and prep for a presentation is to mimic the actual setting and recite the pitch out loud. Saying it out loud will aid in memorization more than reading your notes quietly to yourself. An empty room pitch also allows you to practice your mannerisms and stage presence.

On a side note, I find it more comfortable to sit when I give presentations. You should always do what you feel is most comfortable for you. That being said, you should also respect the customs of different cultures.

Get Feedback, Feedback, Feedback. Get in the habit of pitching in one-on-one settings and asking for feedback. No matter how solid you believe your pitch is, it can always be better. Try to identify the developers around you who have completely different goals and perspectives from yours. The more you test your pitch with these different perspectives, the better you'll be at building presentations with that perspective in mind.

The importance of these soft skills cannot be overstated. Succeeding in them will ensure a more positive design culture on your projects, a culture of idea sharing and collaboration. One with which the developers feel ownership in the experience and drive passion into their work. All of this can be felt in the final product. Ignoring these skills, on the other hand, will generally lead to a project that is dragged across the finish line.

Even more important, perhaps, is the manager's ability to help their designers grow in each skill. Identifying which specific skills need work and building a development plan can turn lackluster designers into star performers. Everyone has potential, but they need the right skills to be successful.

CHAPTER 16

THE ROLE OF A GREAT GAME DESIGNER

There are times where I feel that nothing can prepare you for the reality of this job. At the ninety-day performance review for junior designers, I usually hear the same comment: "I had no idea this is what the job was." Most people aspire to be game designers because they have a passion for games and believe they have great ideas. Those same people will generally have two major misconceptions about the standard day-to-day for game designers:

1. **As a game designer, my great ideas will go into games and make them great.**
   The reality: Game design isn't about ideation. Ideas don't go into games until they are designed out into rules, mechanics, and systems (which is the actual job). Also, making games great takes a lot of iteration and patience. Designs are never plug and play. Your designs will fail more times than they'll succeed. Your job is to keep learning and make the game better with each iteration.

2. **Everyone will respect my ideas and be excited to develop them.**
   The reality: The team is filled with passionate game developers with their own ideas. Your job title isn't what earns you trust and respect. Trust and respect are earned through hard work and by trusting and respecting others. The game belongs to the whole team. All ideas are valid. It's on you to find the right ones through listening and communication.

These two misconceptions end up creating the most conflict between designers and the rest of the team. The designers who succeed understand the reality of the actual role:

> The role of a great game designer is to work with and empower the team to develop a great gameplay experience.

The True Day-to-Day

As game designers, we don't simply design games. We drive the gameplay experience. Designing games is just a part of that job. To drive this point home, I put together a version of the actual day-to-day job for a senior gameplay designer:

10:00 AM: Sync the latest approved dev build. Check your schedule and emails to get ready for the day. You take note of an email thread you should reply to and an afternoon design discussion that you're leading.

- Decide whether the email thread needs an in-person discussion to close it or if one more reply will do the trick. Compose the reply with appropriate images and explanation.

- Open the presentation for the design discussion. Notice a couple of slides still need to be developed. You want to give a couple of design options to the group to start off the discussion and see what the devs respond to. Also, you'll need to make sure the design goals for the feature are appropriate to drive the direction of the discussion.

10:30 AM: Open the latest build to check the current status of the player experience and the features you drive.

- A new AI Archetype is in, but its detection radius is too big, its health seems too high, and its weapon is a bit overpowered (OP). It's hurting the gameplay experience by causing frustration when the player is using standard weapons and tactics against it. The appropriate tactic to beat it isn't working without a lot of skill. You message the AI designer.
- Take notes on other gameplay mechanics and your systems that may need to be fine-tuned.

11:00 AM: Gameplay programmer Patty approaches you with concerns about Mechanic A. She mentions that the current design is running into issues with implementation and asks if you want to go left or right on a decision.

- You first bring up the goals of the design and ask if she still believes in them. She does.
- You ask for her thoughts on whether *she* would go left or right. She brings up issues with each option and seems unhappy about them both. Is she unhappy with the overall design or just the current issue at hand? You learn it's just the current issue.
- You discuss the two options and the pros and cons of each and come to the consensus to create a third option that resolves the issues the first two have. This new solution

could add a major scope risk. Patty seems happier with this option and you ask her to do a tech assessment.

11:30 AM: Sync with the gameplay team. You approach the gameplay developers who focus on the features you're driving. You get a sense of the current status of each feature and see if there are any concerns.

- The junior gameplay designer, Bob, is having issues prototyping his design. You sit with him and ask the intention of the design and his goals. You help him find an easier and faster approach that will prove the goals.

- The lead gameplay programmer, Maya, has already heard about your discussion with Patty and the more costly decision. She has some ideas on how to reduce the cost and has already discussed the approach with Patty. The team seems more confident.

- The lead gameplay animator, Julius, is unhappy with the current gameplay experience. He seems all over the place with his concerns. You ask to continue the discussion over lunch.

12:00 PM: Lunch with lead gameplay animator. While you are walking to the restaurant, the lead goes off on almost every section of the game. His concerns aren't just focused on animation or gameplay.

- You listen to all concerns and take them in, asking questions to ensure you're understanding. You look for a common concern that ties it all together.

- You spot the concern and repeat it back for confirmation: "Your concern is that the player's actions don't feel like they're having an impact on the world. Is that the main issue?" He confirms that issue is the main concern.

- Over lunch you riff on likely causes of the issue and possible solutions. You stress that these areas of the gameplay experience aren't yours (which he understands) but you'll bring it up with the lead game designer and game director. He thanks you for listening. Lunch ends.

1:30 PM: Check emails and messages. The AI designer, Natalie, responded that she knows about the tuning issues and will have it done in the afternoon. Also, the earlier email thread didn't close and there have been many more replies.

- You pull the key stakeholders in that email thread aside to discuss in person, ensuring everyone is aligned with the goals and the problem that needs to be solved.
- The group comes to a consensus on next steps and you ask one of them to own the reply to the full email thread with the plan.

2:00 PM: Design discussion. You're driving this meeting. A few weeks ago, some holes in the gameplay loop were brought up and you've been working out how to solve them. You've invited a few key stakeholders to the discussion as well as some fellow game designers, including your lead. You've developed some goals to kick off this meeting and a couple of example solutions.

- You start by describing the problem. This sparks some discussion but, overall, everyone agrees that this is a problem that needs to be solved. Some think it can be solved with the current feature set.
- You discuss what you believe to be the cause. This cause cannot be solved with the current feature set. You may need a new feature.
- You propose two possible solutions. You stress that these are simple designs meant to spark conversation. The

conversation takes the rest of the hour. The room reaches a consensus to augment an already planned feature to also solve this problem.

- The meeting ends with some developers still not feeling confident in the solution. You take notes to talk to these devs one-on-one later.
- The already planned feature that you'll repurpose is a design you already own. You let everyone know you'll adjust the current prototype for it to see if you can expand it to solve this issue. The meeting adjourns.

3:00 PM: After the meeting, you pull the lead game designer aside and explain the issues brought up over lunch. The lead GD explains that the game director has been looking into similar topics and would want to hear this perspective.

3:30 PM: You sit back at your desk to write up the notes from the design discussion and send out the follow-up email with next steps. Before you can finish, the AI designer stops by to have you check out her tuning for the new AI archetype.

- You head back to her desk where the game is up and running. You play the experience.
- The tuning feels much better, but you believe she may have overcorrected and made it a bit easy. After discussion you agree that her approach may be best for the initial internal playtest.
- You bring up that she may need to retune when the junior gameplay designer's prototyped feature gets implemented. Her eyes go wide and she mentions she's never heard of this feature. Crap.
- You quickly bring her over to the junior gameplay designer, Bob.

4:00 PM: The junior designer has made good progress on the new approach to his prototype.

- The two designers start discussing the purpose of the feature. The junior designer steps through the prototype.
- The AI designer seems nervous and starts questioning the purpose. You help the junior designer explain his points when necessary. The two designers soon find common ground and discuss how to work together to ensure the feature is successful.
- They seem to have everything under control. You excuse yourself so you can head back to your desk.

4:30 PM: You finally get back to your desk and are ready to finish the meeting recap email and start working on your prototype. Instead, the game director stops by. He heard from the lead game designer about your feedback on the gameplay experience.

- You bring him up to speed that most of the feedback came from the lead gameplay animator, Julius. You explain the lunch and the conclusions you reached on the problem at hand.
- The game director agrees and states that it's a big hole between the main differentiator and the game loop. He's been working with the systems designers to figure out opportunities to better drive player motivation. You hash out a few ideas and he asks you to book a meeting with him to discuss it further. He steps away.
- You return to the meeting recap email and send it out. You open your old prototype and try to remember how you put it together.

5:00 PM: Designer sync, a weekly meeting where all the game designers can sync up and discuss what they're up to and any issues that have come to light with the overall gameplay experience.

- Each designer takes their turn stating what they're working on and asking any questions they may have.

- On your turn, you bring up the recent decision to expand a previous design to solve new problems. You ask if there are any concerns with that approach but you're met with silence. Then you state the gameplay experience concerns brought up by the lead gameplay animator. You're following that up with the game director. The UX designer asks to be included in that discussion.

- The lead GD discusses the features that are up for director review later in the week. One of your features is on the list. You'll want to ensure that feature is tuned to your liking before the review meeting.

- Finally, a designer steps up for Show & Tell to showcase what they're working on to get feedback from the entire game design team.

6:00 PM: Back at your desk. You try to finalize everything you started that day and take notes on where to pick things up tomorrow.

- You quickly boot the game to check the feature that the directors will review this week. Everything looks ready. You take note of the build number as a fallback plan for the review in case things break later on in the week.

- You book a meeting with the game director to discuss the gameplay experience concerns raised by the lead gameplay animator. You include the UX designer. You also message the animator to inform him about the meeting and thank him again for the feedback. He's happy he could help and is okay with not being in the meeting.

- You schedule time for yourself to dive deeper into your old prototype.

Each day is filled with distractions and alterations. Problems will surface and you'll be expected to raise any problems you find with their owners. Colleagues will approach you with things they feel are missing or issues they have with the current vision. They will poke holes, pitch alternate ideas, and protest when things aren't fun. *All of this is exactly what you want.* It happens in passionate teams and ensures a better product. But for people who believe being a game designer is about themselves and their ideas, it becomes a rude awakening. These designers will complain and see this input as interruptions and frustrations. They will wish to be left alone to do their job. To them, a game designer is there to tell everyone else what the game will be. These people design games, but are not game designers.

This job isn't for everyone. Every step of the way is a constant collaborative effort. If you believe your design is best then it's on you to convince and inspire everyone, not just expect them to fall in line. And they won't simply fall in line a majority of the time. The more people there are on the team, the more passion there is all around you. But these developers are passionate about games and about the industry, not about you and your ideas.

But if you can lead, if you can inspire, if you see every nay-saying developer as an opportunity and not a pain, then you'll not only succeed but thrive. You'll be able to turn their passion into something working with you instead of against you. And the games you develop will thrive as well.

Helpful Tips

The following are my top tips for quick reference. As you hit roadblocks on projects, with peers, or with your career, refer to these:

- **Ask the Golden Question**: What's the problem you're trying to solve? This question has saved me more than anything else in my career. It helps keep my designs focused and helps to reveal why others are excited about the ideas they're pitching. Every feature is solving a problem in the current experience. If it isn't, then why are you adding it?

- **Build belief in a design** by ensuring the team agrees that (a) there's a problem, (b) it needs to be solved, and (c) X is the optimal solution (in that order).

- **Turn your biggest skeptics into your greatest advocates.** Never shy away from your biggest adversaries (and try not to fire them either). Game development requires passionate devs and a perfect mix of conflict and harmony. It's on the design team to ensure that balance. The loudest voices fighting your vision can quickly become your biggest advocates. Simply listening, understanding, and discussing their goals will go a long way toward developing a powerful solution together.

- **Be the last one to speak in a meeting.** This not only ensures you're listening and taking in all points of view, but it ensures you aren't stomping others as well.

- **Start with intuition and end with logic.** That gut feeling can be wrong a lot when it comes to creative fields in which every feature has different goals and every project has a different vision. Dig deeper to determine why that gut feeling was triggered and discuss the actual concerns or conclusions that caused those feelings.

YOU CAN DO THIS! It's very easy for the industry to beat you down and make you jaded. Crunch, canceled projects, poor reviews, and closed studios can do that to anyone. First and foremost, take care of yourself and the others around you. Your health and the relationships you build will always be more important than any game. You've got this.

In Closing

The exact role of a game designer changes among different studios, projects, and design specialties. My goal with this book was to shine light on the core expectations and requirements of every game designer in the industry. Some positions may require more skills that I haven't covered, but there's no doubt in my mind that, if you master the areas highlighted in this book, you'll be able to excel at any game designer position in the industry. Good luck out there.

AFTERWORD

Writing this book has been a tougher challenge than I could have imagined—not just with writing the content, but with editing it. There comes a point where you just have to let go of the idea that it will be perfect.

At first, this series was meant to be one larger book. But as I crossed the two hundred–page mark with this installment I knew I had to break it out into smaller titles, with the hopes of saving the reader and my own sanity.

My first Game Developers Conference (GDC) talk, *Designing Your Design Team,* was created to examine a problem I'd seen countless times in my career. My goal was to start a discussion, see if others had noticed the same problem, and propose a solution. That one talk triggered many responses, and I found myself overjoyed to continue the conversation through emails and message boards. I realized that most designers were creating talks about their specific projects and post-mortems. Not many were looking at the industry as a whole and identifying teamwide and studiowide problems. These types of problems have been pushing me to create more GDC talks and write this book series. Thank you to everyone who has messaged me to keep the conversation alive. Each message I've received has reinvigorated me.

It's my hope that my readers get something positive out of this book: a better understanding of the complexities of being a game designer. The job is not easy, but I hope this book has better equipped you for the task. The industry will evolve, and this role will evolve with it. This is just the start of the conversation.

Coming Soon

Book 2: Embracing Different Design Perspectives

Book 3: Building a Career as a Game Designer

Book 4: Ensuring a Positive, Collaborative Design Culture

Please visit www.gamedesignerhandbook.com for more information on upcoming books and talks or to schedule the author for a speaking event.

ACKNOWLEDGMENTS

Thank you for the feedback and support: Katya Garipova, Michael Wasilewski, Michael Surya, Avi Mintz, Richard Schwartz, Mathieu Berube, Nicolas Hesler, Ahmed Ghoneim, Rachel Lowery, Sarah Lane, Mahadev Rojas Torres.

Thank you for the mentorship & friendship throughout my career: Colleen Wheeler, Jackie Shuler, Edward Dorsey, Jeff Ecker, Mo Kakwan, Eunice Chen, Kudo Tsunoda, Zak Phelps, Darren Bennett, Steve Latta, Liam Millar, Ryan Seekley, Dan Machen, David Press, Mark Gorski, Christophe Labrune, Josh Tsui, Wylie Robinson, Kerry Hermann, Chelsea Blasko, Tom Farnsworth, Chuck Beaver, Glen Schofield, Michael Condrey, Bret Robbins, Ian Milham, Jatin Patel, Dino Ignacio, Jason Leong, John Geraci, Peter Iliev, Tracy Espeleta Ho, Joey Spiotto, Bonnie Rosenstein, John Gabriel, Jeremy Ñatividad, Kacper Centkowski, David Kuo, Matthew Talma, Sachin Pansuria, Dave Votypka, Erin Daly, Brian Holinka, Martin Raymond, Robert Ryan, Keith Alexander, Dante Rinaldi, Bill Millard, Zhuo "Chuck" Deng, Hougant Chen, Jon Uy, Eric Bryant, Avi Mintz, Vitoria Lee, Chris Williams, Jade Raymond, Alex Parizeau, Heather Holmes, Scott Lee, Pat Redding, Andy Wilson, Lesley Phord-Toy, Laurent Malville, Michael Wasilewski, Kristjan Zadziuk, Josh Cook, Cindy Cook, Kent Wilson, Rick Hoskinson, Matt Rose,

Liam Gilbride, Lathieeshe Thillainathan, Dan Ebanks, Sam Cross, Zack Cooper, Rima Brek, Robyn Smith, Heather Steele, David Grivel, Alex Luffman, Michael Surya, David Yorke, Nitai Bessete, Travis McGill, Michelle Rudson, Andrew Rudson, Jon Paul Schelter, Chris Nesbitt, Feargus Carroll, Olexiy Zhukov-Malyeyev, Hugh Norfolk, Jensen Verlaan, Laura Hoeltzenbein, Raymond Graham, Matt Severin, Peter Handrinos, Navid Khavari, Shawn Carroll, Yannick Spagna, Farid El-Namr, Latham Bromwich, Margherita Seconnino, Thomas Singleton, Dan Soltyka, Sherry Zhou, Jesse Knapp, Eduardo Hulshof, Aaron Gordon, Ben Millwood, Emily Claire Afan, Justin Del Giudice, Paolo Pace, Dan Cox, Braydon Beaulieu, Aaron Halon, and many more.

Thank you for the love & support throughout my life: Edward Carrillo, Maria Melendez, Edward Carrillo Jr, Irma Carrillo, Silvia Camacho, Louis Camacho, Rosalind Rodriguez, Emiliano Rodriguez, Nancy Romo, Octavio Romo, Irma Parada, Justina Castro, Crystal Cornejo, Camille Mejia, Daniel Rodriguez, Felicia Camacho, Nick Parada, Clemente Rodriguez, Nita Jacome, Gayle Carrillo, Nic Filzen, Patrick Oedewaldt, Bill Scott, Joe Bennett, Jesse Vance, Robert Hanson, Mike Weaver, Derik Marcussen, Mike DeTrempe, Tony Pagán, Erin Holly, Derek Barlow, Christina Holt, Brandon Bronson, Matt Davis, Lionel Jackson, Erin (Hobbs) McMurray, Dan Weidner, Jared Koberstein, Adam Rosenberger, Saima Nawaz, Brian Carroll, Matt Alden, Mark Cochran, Jeff Griffin, Mark Miller, Rich Walther, Catherine Sheu, Trish Simpson, Kelly Brown, and many more.

Thank you to the readers and game devs who make this industry great.

SNEAK PEAK OF *BOOK 2:* *DESIGN PERSPECTIVES*

In *Book 1: The Role of a Great Game Designer,* I defined game design, discussed the design process, and talked about the core skills game designers need. But I didn't go too deep into how to turn ideas into designs. More specifically, I haven't yet discussed how designers should approach their fantasy, mechanics, systems, or player goals in order to create captivating designs. I've mentioned that every design is a problem to solve but have not yet covered the perspective one should take when designing the creative solution.

I haven't discussed this for one main reason:

> Informing someone how to go about creative thinking is counterintuitive to creativity and can stifle unique perspectives.

Anyone who says that you should consider design from a specific perspective is really just expressing how it works for them. But will that work for you? If you force yourself to think their way, you are suppressing your own creativity and reducing the impact your perspective could have on the design.

During my career, I've seen different games from one publisher come out feeling the same because the publisher mandated how designers should approach the creative process of design. The positive effect was that all designers and developers shared a common vocabulary when discussing design and could more easily work through problems together. But creative environments require both conflict and harmony. By mandating specific perspectives, conflict was reduced, but each game, even when made by different studios, started to showcase the same systems and gameplay loops despite having different fantasies and genres. At the same time, we saw other companies take our formulas to new heights by applying a different perspective to them.

The goal of every creative venture should be to foster creative diversity and not stifle it. We need to embrace how differently everyone thinks and not create processes that require one way of creative thinking.

The Four Design Perspectives

When solving design problems, what types of questions do you ask yourself first? What do you feel needs to work before everything else falls into place? What emotional or gameplay experiences do you prioritize? Hopefully by the end of this chapter you can confidently answer these questions about yourself. And even better, as you master your understanding of these perspectives, you'll be able to answer these questions about the other designers around you.

Every time we solve a problem in our lives or in game development, we are gaining experience. Not only are we better equipped to solve similar problems in the future, but we also become better equipped to solve problems in general. Just like any other skill, problem solving takes practice. And the more practice we have the more we start to solidify our approach to problem solving. For example, if you flip a light switch and the light doesn't turn on, what do you do? Chances are your first thought will go to whatever solution has worked most often in your recent years. For some that's checking the plug, for others it's the bulb, but for me it's the master switch by the front door.

The light switch example is oversimplified in that it's not a creative problem. Design fields are creative endeavors so there's an added layer of culture, artistry, and subjectivity. Designers will approach creative problem solving from the perspective that personally excites them the most as well as in light of whatever has worked well for them in the past. These two considerations are generally linked since we almost always start with our preferred perspective. This is why conflict is always needed in creative environments: Building experiences from the same perspective will only take us so far.

Throughout my career I've noticed patterns in the game designers I've worked with—patterns with what they liked or disliked, patterns in how they approached problems. Sometimes this helped me to better understand the designers around me and allowed me to adjust my approaches. Sometimes this led to conflicts that I could not understand how to avoid. It was my failure to understand certain designers that led me to search for the reasons why. The usual instinct is to believe that they are bad at their jobs and we are good. But I knew this couldn't be the case. Their resumes alone showed that much. So I started to dive deeper into the patterns of the designers around me. Categorizing them and questioning their methods revealed the four design perspectives.

Everything in this section of the book is based on my theory of the four design perspectives. This theory can be applied to any field of design. It's something I've used to better understand myself and the other designers around me. It's helped me to structure teams and task designers to ensure their success. The four design perspectives are based on the different approaches one can have when exploring an experience or problem: high level, low level, bottom up and top down.

High Level vs. Low Level
I consider these two approaches to be the production methods of design. They focus on your approach to building the design and developing the product.

High-Level Design. This method requires a broader look at the entire experience. It's focused on pillars, structure, emotion, or goals. Typically, high-level design is more concerned with the experience as a whole or larger components of it—conceptualizing how everything comes together or the common link everything is tied to.

For example, if you're designing a commercial, what type of emotion do you want the consumer to feel about the product? What's the overall message you want them walking away with? What are the brand guidelines that need to be reflected? High-level design focuses on selling the client and the team on the overall dream.

Low-Level Design. This method has a more specific focus on individual components and how things operate. It searches for detail rather than overview, exploring how each specific piece will be experienced. Low-level design is generally more focused on quick iteration of the experience rather than on long conceptualization.

Using the same commercial example, low-level design will focus on the individual set pieces, script, and casting. What's the specific tag line or jingle that could be catchy? Can we create five options quickly, see which ones the client likes, and then iterate?

These two approaches are always at odds. Both are needed, but which should take priority? With high-level design, you'd prefer to get your ducks in a row before pulling the trigger, but the risk is that, after you're done, you still don't have a product. With low-level design you're quickly iterating on the product but running the risk that all the pieces may not come together into a singular message. You may end up with a lot of individual pieces that work well on their own but not together.

Both of these approaches are necessary to ensure a quality product. Each must be done while considering the other. It's important to note that the smaller your experience, the more these two approaches are one and the same. Game design students often have trouble understanding high-level design as their experiences are usually smaller prototypes of individual systems. But the larger your experience, the more issues you'll see if either approach is missing.

Bottom up vs. Top Down

I consider these two approaches to be run-time methods of design. As you step through the experience mentally or physically, whose eyes are you seeing the experience from?

Bottom-up Design. This method is always considering the experience from the user's perspective, moving through it as the user would, looking at components based on how the user will interact with them and how they're feeling when they experience it. What does the user feel? What can the user do?

For example, when designing a website's interface, this approach will always be thinking of UX. Will the user be able to discover how to add things to their cart? How many clicks does it take to purchase the item? How can we enhance the usability of the site while still maintaining the amount of information and options it contains?

Top-Down Design. This method breaks down the experience from the system's perspective, taking a behind-the-scenes look at how systems play out and interact with each other to create the experience. When System A is engaged, how do Systems B and C react? With this approach, the user is just another catalyst that the systems react to.

Using the same website example, this approach focuses on what happens behind the scenes. What happens when the user purchases an item? Where does all that information go? What if they didn't fill out a field that's needed? What if the credit card data aren't valid? What if the item is out of stock? What are all the possible errors that could occur with these systems and how do we handle them? How do we optimize the systems and ensure they flow unimpeded?

These two approaches are also at odds, but both are needed for the optimal experience. Focusing only on bottom-up design may push toward a great user experience but it may also reduce the systems to the point where the experience feels shallow. Focusing only on top down may create truly innovative systems and simulations but sacrifice the user's ability to discover and understand the depth available.

Similar to high-level vs. low-level, with these approaches, the smaller your experience the more you may not notice a difference between them. In Rock, Paper, Scissors, the user experience and systems experience are nearly identical because all are tied to one system. But the more complex your experience, the more you'll notice a vast difference between these two viewpoints.

These four viewpoints form a spectrum of how designers can perceive an experience or approach a problem that needs to be solved. This spectrum can be expressed in the following quadrant chart of design perspectives:

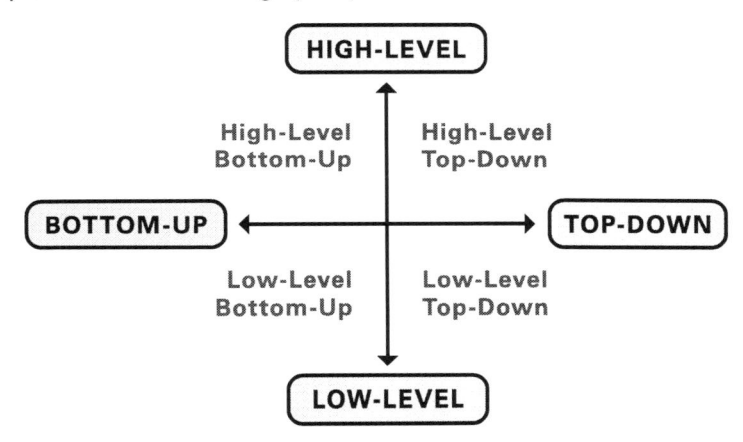

```
                    ┌─────────────┐
                    │ HIGH-LEVEL  │
                    └─────────────┘
                           ▲
          High-Level       │       High-Level
          Bottom-Up        │       Top-Down
┌───────────┐              │              ┌──────────┐
│ BOTTOM-UP │◄─────────────┼─────────────►│ TOP-DOWN │
└───────────┘              │              └──────────┘
          Low-Level        │       Low-Level
          Bottom-Up        │       Top-Down
                           ▼
                    ┌─────────────┐
                    │  LOW-LEVEL  │
                    └─────────────┘
```

But let's refocus these terms specifically for game design to give us a better understanding on what this means for game designers:

> **High-Level Design → Direction:** Direction is conceptual. Direction is what the experience hopes to accomplish and become. It is the vision that all features should stem from. What is our world? What is the game's purpose? What is the player's purpose within the game? Direction is focused on *goals, vision, concepts, emotion,* and *motivations.*
>
> **Low-Level Design → Gameplay:** Gameplay is physical. Gameplay is how the players and systems engage with each other to create the experience. It is the feature set that comes together to become the game. What can

the player do? How does the world react? Gameplay is focused on engagement and the input and output of the experience.

Bottom-up Design → Player: The player is our user and the external source of the experience. Designing for the player means running through the experience from the player's viewpoint. Who are they as a player, what is their avatar, what can they see, how can they interact with the world? The player experience is focused mainly on *play, interaction, discoverability,* and *understanding.*

Top-Down Design → Systems: The systems are our structure and the internal source of the experience. Designing for systems means stepping through the experience from the systems' viewpoint. How does the world behave? How does it react to external forces? How does it ramp up to increase challenge? The systems experience is focused mainly on *structure, challenge,* and *balance.*

Adjusting our terminology for game design creates the following spectrum of perspectives:

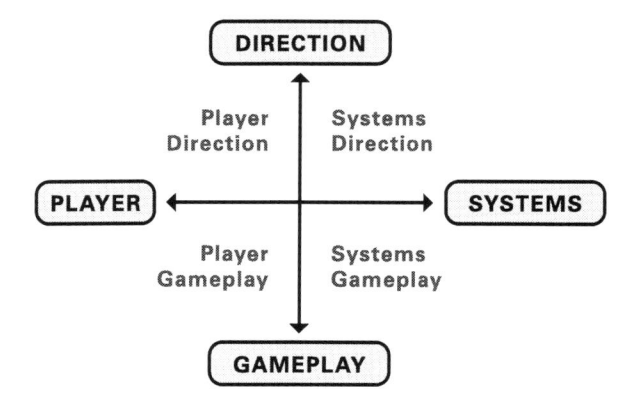

```
                    DIRECTION
                        ↑
         Player      |   Systems
         Direction   |   Direction
                    |
  PLAYER  ←─────────┼─────────→  SYSTEMS
                    |
         Player      |   Systems
         Gameplay    |   Gameplay
                        ↓
                    GAMEPLAY
```

In turn, these perspectives give us the four game designer types:

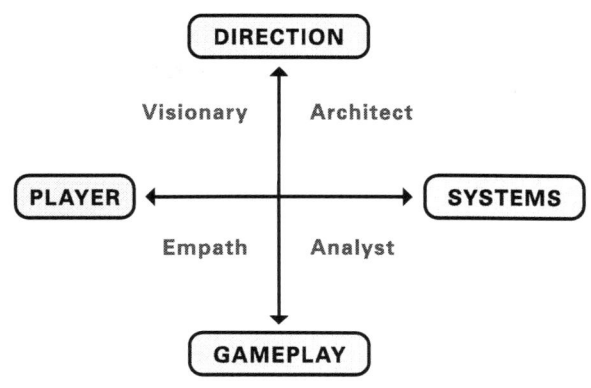

```
                    DIRECTION
                        ↑
         Visionary  |  Architect
                    |
   PLAYER ←─────────┼─────────→ SYSTEMS
                    |
          Empath    |  Analyst
                        ↓
                    GAMEPLAY
```

Our goal in identifying these four types isn't to pigeonhole designers. It's simply to help us understand each other's perspectives. Too often have I walked away from an exchange with another designer, completely lost as to what they were saying and wondering why they thought their proposed approach was any good. I didn't understand where they were coming from or their perspective. As you better understand these four game designer types and the types of designers around you, you'll be able to have more meaningful conversations about design and reduce negative conflicts. And ensuring you have all four designer types on your team will ensure you'll still have the positive conflict needed to find the optimal solution.

Also, when you understand the designer types and the game you're making, you'll be better equipped to build an appropriate design team. Most studios lean heavily toward one or two designer types, and this can be felt in their games. *Eve Online* (CCP Games, 2003) and *World of Tanks* (Wargaming, 2010) are very systems-focused experiences and come from systems-focused studios. *Journey* (Thatgamecompany, 2012) is very player focused and, more specifically, Visionary focused. That studio tends to think about the emotional experience they want to develop as early as possible. Studios that push for mass-market games will generally want to build teams that cover all four designer types. This ensures their games are more well-rounded in order to serve a larger number of different markets.

There is no right or wrong perspective, but understanding who is on your team will give you insights into what the end product will look like. It can also help you understand why a specific designer-feature pairing may not be working out. For example, if I want a hardcore, balanced economy with multiple currencies, then it's in my best interest to task an Analyst rather than a Visionary or Empath. When we think of our design teams, some of this may seem obvious as we know who is better at economy tuning. But diving deeper into understanding these four perspectives will help to reveal not only successful tasking opportunities but also why certain conflicts exist between designers.

About the Author

Richard Carrillo has more than fifteen years' experience in game design. He developed his skills at studios all over North America including EA Tiburon, EA Chicago, EA Redwood Shores, KAOS Studios, Ubisoft Toronto, and Sledgehammer Games Toronto. Working at so many different locations with different principles has taught him unique insights into the game development process and studio structures. With this knowledge and experience, Richard has dedicated himself not only to making great games, but also to bettering the hiring practices, improving the design culture, and developing the skills of game designers across the industry.

Game credits: *Def Jam: ICON, Dead Space, Dead Space 2, Homefront, Tom Clancy's Splinter Cell: Blacklist, Starlink: Battle for Atlas*

You can connect with Richard on:

https://www.gamedesignerhandbook.com

https://twitter.com/Carrillo_GD

https://www.linkedin.com/in/carrillo-gd

Printed in Great Britain
by Amazon